Orchids

for every home

Orchids

for every home

the beginner's guide to
growing beautiful, easy-
care orchids

wilma and brian rittershausen

photography derek cranch

Reader's
Digest

The Reader's Digest Association, Inc.
Pleasantville, New York/Montreal

A READER'S DIGEST BOOK
This edition published by The Reader's Digest Association by arrangement with Toucan Books, Ltd.

Copyright © 2004 Toucan Books Ltd.
Text copyright © 2004 Wilma and Brian Rittershausen

FOR TOUCAN BOOKS
Design: Bradbury and Williams
Editor: Gwen Rigby
Managing Editor: Ellen Dupont
Index: Mary-Jane Steer
Picture Researcher: Christine Vincent
Proofreader: Theresa Bebbington
Cover photograph: Derek Cranch

FOR READER'S DIGEST
U.S. Project Editor: Susan Randol
Canadian Project Editor: Pamela Johnson
Project Designer: George McKeon
Creative Director: Michele Laseau
Executive Editor, Trade Publishing: Dolores York
Associate Publisher, Trade Publishing: Christopher T. Reggio
Vice President & Publisher, Trade Publishing, Harold Clarke

Library of Congress Cataloging-in-Publication Data:
Rittershausen, Wilma.
Orchids for every home : the beginner's guide to growing beautiful, easy-care orchids /
Wilma and Brian Rittershausen
 p. cm.
Includes index.
ISBN 0-7621-0491-0 (Hardcover)
ISBN 978-1-60652-205-9 (Paperback)
 1. Orchid culture. 2. Orchids. I. Rittershausen, Brian II. Title

SB409.R565 2004
635.9'344–dc22   2003058755

Address any comments about Orchids for Every Home to:
The Reader's Digest Association, Inc.
Adult Trade Publishing
44 S. Broadway
White Plains, NY 10601

NOTE TO OUR READERS
This publication contains the opinions and ideas of its authors and is designed to provide useful information to the reader. It is not intended as a substitute for the advice of an expert on the subject matter covered. Products or active ingredients, treatments, and the names of organizations that appear in this publication are included for informational purposes only; the inclusion of commercial products in the book does not imply endorsement by Reader's Digest. When using any commercial product, readers should read and follow all label directions carefully.

The authors and publisher specifically disclaim any responsibility for any liability, loss, or risk (personal, financial, or otherwise) that may be claimed or incurred as a consequence—directly or indirectly—of the use and/or application of any of the contents of this publication.

For more Reader's Digest products and information, visit our website:
www.rd.com (in the United States)

Printed in Singapore
1 3 5 7 9 10 8 6 4 2

preface

When we followed in our father's footsteps over 50 years ago, little did we realize how far our careers in orchids would take us, or how, in this half century, orchids would rise in prominence to become the universally popular houseplants of today. Modern practices of mass propagation that have brought orchids into the limelight and the rush of new, easy-to-grow varieties existed only in our imaginations, well beyond our wildest dreams. In particular, the phenomenal rise of the phalaenopsis from a temperamental greenhouse occupant to a windowsill favorite has been amazing. Fifty years ago orchids were expensive and limited to those fortunate enough to own a greenhouse. Now they are within everyone's reach, available globally through many different outlets, satisfying what has become an insatiable desire to own and grow these most beautiful and fascinating of tropical plants.

In this introductory book, we describe only those orchids that have gained favor for growing as houseplants, both in warm and cool climates. These are the undeniably showiest varieties with instant flower appeal that often succeed where ordinary plants fail. We have not mentioned any of the lesser-known types, often referred to as botanical orchids. These are even more numerous than those described here, but belong in the specialist's collection, or in their native home.

The information we give is based on our own experience of growing orchids, and is offered as guidance that will lead the enthusiast to a basic knowledge. Experience comes with time, and as you acquire further knowledge and understanding of these remarkable plants, you too may aspire to seek out more wonders among the orchid family.

It is our sincere hope that this book will inspire and assist you to make your wildest orchid dreams come true.

Wilma and Brian Rittershausen

contents

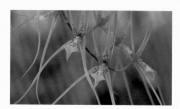

the orchid

Orchids have never been so plentiful or so cheap. Comparable in price to a bouquet of cut flowers or ordinary potted plants, an orchid represents far better value because it will last longer in flower. If properly cared for, it will live for many years. Orchids all grow easily somewhere in the world, but not all of them grow together in the same climate. There are orchids from temperate zones and some from tropical climates. As houseplants, they need different conditions to succeed.

Orchid (or-kid)

A plant of the family *Orchidaceae*. The flowers are of unusual shapes and gorgeous colors. There are an estimated 25,000 wild species and 1,400 genera. They grow worldwide.

all about the orchid

For millions of years, orchid species abounded in the world's tropical rain forests. Now man-made hybrids, which are the descendants of these plants, grace our living rooms and gardens in ever greater numbers and ever more exciting varieties.

Orchids belong to a huge family of plants called *Orchidaceae*. What separates them from all other plant families is the way they package their pollen in small waxy bundles called pollinia, for collection by visiting insects. By this unique system, no pollen grains are lost. Instead, the insects carry pollen from one orchid to another, thereby fertilizing their flowers.

Orchids are separated into groups according to their botanical similarities. These groups—*Phalaenopsis* and *Miltoniopsis*, for example—are called genera. Within each genus are the species—such as *Phalaenopsis sanderiana* and *Miltoniopsis vexillaria*. Hybrids are made by breeding between the species and also by combining two or more genera to make intergeneric hybrids. Since orchids interbreed so readily, more easily than any other family in the plant kingdom, a multitude of hybrids is now available.

WHAT'S IN A NAME?

If you are not sure if a plant is a species or a hybrid, check the label. For example, the most commonly available species of *Pleione* is *Pleione formosana*, named for the island of Formosa, which is where it comes from. Where the second name is latinized like this, the plant is a species. Hybrid plants are given non-latinized names such as *Pleione* Shantung.

ODONTOGLOSSUM TYPE

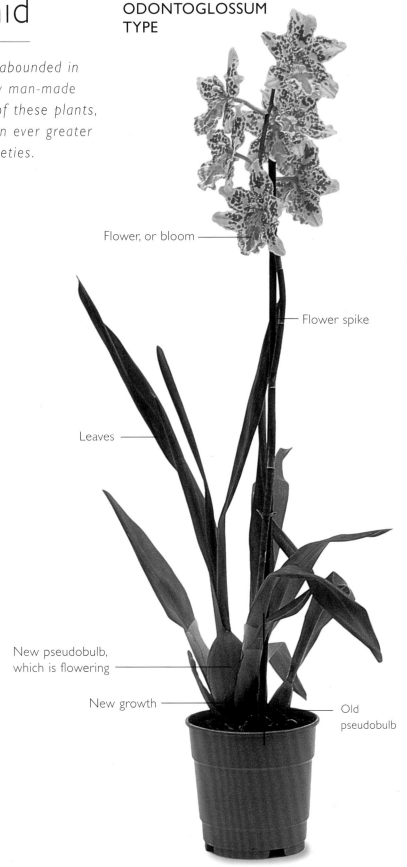

Flower, or bloom

Flower spike

Leaves

New pseudobulb, which is flowering

New growth

Old pseudobulb

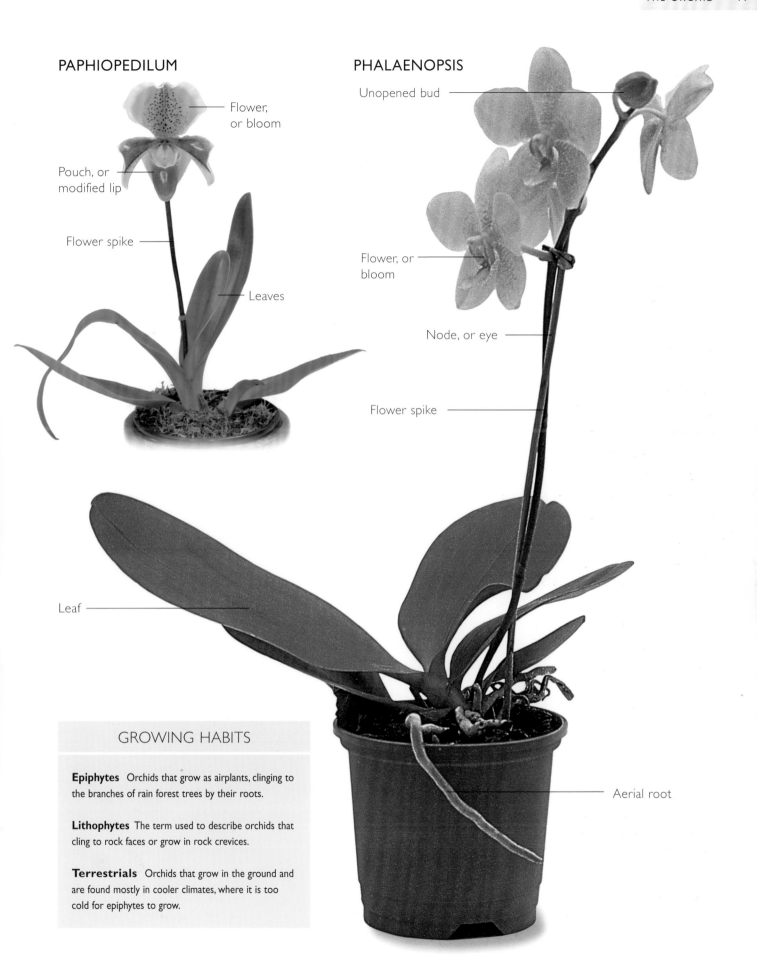

PAPHIOPEDILUM

Flower, or bloom

Pouch, or modified lip

Flower spike

Leaves

PHALAENOPSIS

Unopened bud

Flower, or bloom

Node, or eye

Flower spike

Leaf

Aerial root

GROWING HABITS

Epiphytes Orchids that grow as airplants, clinging to the branches of rain forest trees by their roots.

Lithophytes The term used to describe orchids that cling to rock faces or grow in rock crevices.

Terrestrials Orchids that grow in the ground and are found mostly in cooler climates, where it is too cold for epiphytes to grow.

orchid flowers

All flowering plants are classified by the shape of their blooms. Orchids conform to a standard pattern—three outside sepals, two inside petals, and a lip, the third or central petal. The pollinating parts are in the center. Within this blueprint each orchid has its individual characteristics. For example, all the segments of brassias are long and thin, while the lip on the miltoniopsis is the largest part of the flower. Here are a few common and distinctive blooms.

Miniature
Phalaenopsis

Standard candy-striped *Phalaenopsis*

Phragmipedium

Vanda

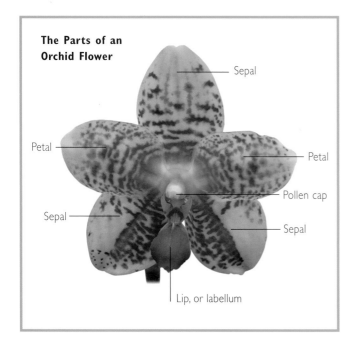

The Parts of an Orchid Flower

Sepal

Petal

Petal

Sepal

Pollen cap

Sepal

Lip, or labellum

Cymbidium

Miltoniopsis

Zygopetalum

Single color
Odontoglossum

Soft-caned
Dendrobium

Brassia

Oncidium

Patterned
Odontoglossum

Hard-caned
Dendrobium

growing orchids indoors

Orchids will grow almost anywhere in the house. Find out what conditions your orchids need and try to provide them. When you get the conditions right, long-lasting blooms will be your reward.

DO'S
✔ Keep orchids away from direct sources of heat such as radiators and even the television.
✔ Keep orchids out of cold drafts caused by open windows when the temperature outside is low.
✔ Stand orchids on a humidity tray to make sure that some moisture is always rising around them.

DON'TS
✘ Do not try to grow orchids that need cool and warm temperatures side by side. Give each orchid the range of temperatures that it needs.
✘ Do not expose orchid foliage to direct sun. Keep the plants shaded in the summer in a well-lit area.
✘ Do not try to grow an orchid in a dark, unlit corner of the room.

Growing orchids in your home is easier than in a greenhouse. In a greenhouse, conditions have to be created and maintained to suit the orchids and there are many dangers, from overheating in summer to a heater breakdown in winter. Of course, when it's all working smoothly, the results are optimum growth for the plants in a specially created, ideal environment.

Orchids living in your home are expected to grow in an environment that already exists and that has been designed to suit you. Conditions are often less than perfect. While this puts some restrictions on the range of types you can grow, many orchids are able to adapt.

An indoor growing case can provide orchids with their own microclimate. Artificial lighting can be incorporated, while humidity can be maintained by keeping water in the trays. In northern regions, where light levels are low, this type of case is very useful.

Which room?

Each room in the house can be considered a potential growing area for your orchids. The best places are those rooms in which you spend a good amount of time. Orchids confined to the spare back bedroom will be seldom visited and so may suffer from neglect. Bathrooms are out because the temperature fluctuates rapidly when they are in use. So choose a living room or kitchen, where the temperature is not constant, but varies between night and day by about 63°F (17°C) throughout the year. For the cool-growing types, such as odontoglossums, this means a winter minimum temperature of about 50°F (10°C). The types that prefer warmer conditions, such as phalaenopsis, need a minimum temperature some 10°F (5°C) higher, and a maximum daytime temperature of 80°F (27°C). Any temperature between these two extremes will be suitable.

Creating humidity

Choose a windowsill or other area where there is enough space to stand a humidity tray, which should be larger than the base of the pots you intend to put on it. Place horticultural pellets or similar material, such as gravel, on the base of the tray to a depth of 1 inch (2.5 cm) and pour in enough water to wet half this material. Stand the orchids above the wet base, making sure that they are not standing in the water. If there is room, set small, slow-growing plants—for example, miniature ferns—alongside the orchids. This helps create a humid growing habitat. Once or twice a year, remove the base material, put it into a fine sieve, and wash it thoroughly with a hose or under the faucet.

Shade and light

During the summer, most orchids will thrive as long as they are out of direct midday sun; move them to a windowsill that gets more sun for the winter. Ideally, they need early morning or late afternoon sun in the summer and almost full sun in the winter. Keep orchids such as phalaenopsis and paphiopedilums, which prefer more shade, inside the room, farther away from the window.

Watering and feeding

While orchids are growing, keep them evenly moist. Do not let them dry out completely or become too wet and sodden. Water more in the summer, when the plants dry out more quickly, and much less in the winter. Feed them at every second or third watering while the orchids are growing. If available, use a special orchid feed; otherwise any houseplant food, diluted to half-strength, will do. Overfeeding will leave a residue of chemicals in the compost that will burn the roots.

Growing and resting

When you can see a new leaf appearing, the orchid is growing. When there is no sign of any new leaves, the plant is resting. Some orchids hardly rest at all, while others will remain dormant for several weeks. Orchids that are resting need little water because their roots cannot take it up. If you water orchids at this time, you risk rotting their roots.

WATERING TIPS

◆ Do not let the plants dry out during the growing season.

◆ Submerge the orchid in its pot in a bucket of water until bubbles stop rising.

◆ Orchids on bark dry out fast and may need a daily dip in soft water, with fertilizer added once a week.

◆ Water from the rim of the pot with a spouted watering can.

◆ Water should be at room temperature.

◆ Never let the plants stand in water.

CHOOSING THE CORRECT COMPOST

Orchid compost varies around the world, but it must be soil-free. It must also provide swift drainage and be well aerated so that the roots of the plant can breathe. Among the most common potting materials are various grades of fir bark compost and Rockwool.

Fir bark is a natural substance, while Rockwool is an inert, man-made material. Organic composts like fir bark usually break down, releasing nutrients as they do so, but as

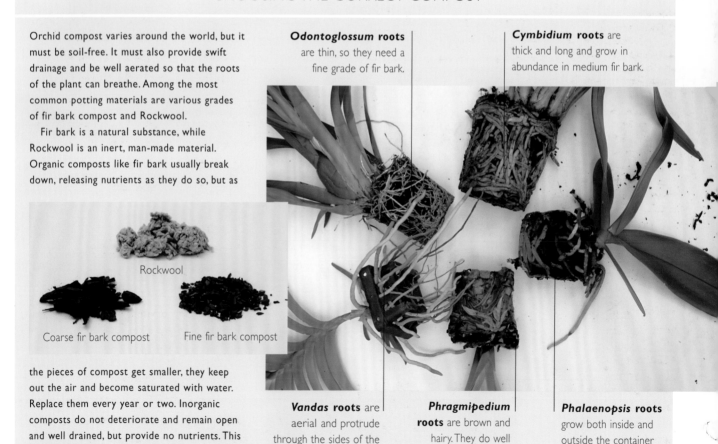

Odontoglossum roots are thin, so they need a fine grade of fir bark.

Cymbidium roots are thick and long and grow in abundance in medium fir bark.

Rockwool

Coarse fir bark compost

Fine fir bark compost

the pieces of compost get smaller, they keep out the air and become saturated with water. Replace them every year or two. Inorganic composts do not deteriorate and remain open and well drained, but provide no nutrients. This means that, except when the orchid is resting, you must feed it regularly with orchid fertilizer.

Vandas roots are aerial and protrude through the sides of the basket, so they need only a little coarse compost.

Phragmipedium roots are brown and hairy. They do well in Rockwool-type compost.

Phalaenopsis roots grow both inside and outside the container and need a medium grade of fir bark.

buying orchids

Orchids can be bought in many different outlets, from grocery stores to garden centers. Buy your orchids as soon as they appear in the stores, when they are fresh from the nursery, and the blooms will last for weeks.

Fully open blossoms, with no buds to come, mean that the flowers are already past their prime, with not much longer to live.

Choosing your first orchid is an exciting experience. The more you shop around, the more aware you will become of the huge selection available. As with all plants, your orchid will originally have been produced from seed or by tissue culture, a procedure where a few single cells have been taken from a mother plant and mass-produced in a laboratory.

Mericloning

In the past, a nurseryman would raise his own plants, growing them through all the stages of development and retailing them directly to his customers. Today, things are very different. Methods of mass propagation, known as mericloning, have led to an unparalleled number of orchids being raised in vast commercial nurseries. Only the best varieties are chosen when the meristem tip, or nucleus of growing cells, is removed from the plant and cultured in laboratories. Huge laboratories produce millions of plants each year.

While young, these plants are sold to a grower who will take them to near flowering size. They will be passed on again to yet another nurseryman, who will bring them into bloom. Finally, they will be sold to a retail outlet. From start to finish, the plants may have traveled half way around the world before reaching a store near you.

Orchids everywhere

Whether you are shopping in a supermarket or garden center, you will find orchids readily available, but with little information on how to look after them. Usually sold under their generic name only

TO SHOP BY NAME OR NOT?

This book gives the full name of the orchids illustrated, but when shopping around, you will discover that many plants are sold with just a generic name, or even no label at all.

Over the years, retail outlets have found that most people want to buy a pink, white, or yellow-flowered variety and that the name is not important or necessary. Names are, however, used by growers and specialist nurseries. But you may have trouble when you try to buy an orchid by name—it may no longer be available!

Every year orchid producers bring out new varieties. In their search for something bigger, better, longer lasting, and more colorful than what was offered last year, new orchids are brought onto the market and old ones disappear. The result is that a named variety, such as *Phalaenopsis* Golden Hat, may stay on the market for only a couple of years at the most before being superseded by a newer model. Check with the supplier to find the nearest orchid among the new hybrids to the one you want.

(for instance, *Phalaenopsis*), they come with a care card giving basic temperature and watering advice.

Buying from a specialist nursery can give you a head start because an experienced grower can give you extra information on fertilizing, light, and temperature requirements. If you don't live near a nursery, try looking for orchids on the World Wide Web. You will find details of mail-order suppliers who are prepared to pack and dispatch orchids over long distances. You will probably be able to find an orchid society near you and it, in turn, will have its own web site. The members are generally amateur growers who will be willing to help an enthusiastic beginner.

Choosing an orchid

Without doubt, the most popular orchid for the last two decades has been the *Phalaenopsis*, and it seems certain to continue as the number one houseplant in many countries for the foreseeable future.

The orchids in this book are listed in order of popularity, so we begin with *Phalaenopsis* which, as the most popular orchid, is usually the most widely available. The types of orchids on sale will vary, depending on location, climate, and the orchid's season. The orchids that have a season will be obtainable at different times of the year—usually when they are about to come into bloom.

Knowing what to look for

The plant will have been fit and healthy when it left the grower, but if conditions have not been right since then, the buds may be yellow and shriveled. These will drop off and the plant should be avoided. Other problems may occur with the foliage

and roots; you can spot these problems if you look carefully at the plant (see below).

When you buy your orchid, ask the sales staff if they have any growing information for you. Even a short leaflet will help you with its care.

Long-term beauty

With the increased popularity of orchids as houseplants, many people buy them, enjoy the flowers, and then throw the plants away. This is a waste because an orchid can live for a very long time. With the correct care and attention, it will continue to flower and re-flower in its season, giving immense pleasure over several years.

Flower spikes Make sure that they are staked correctly and that some buds are unopened.

When buying your orchid, examine the plant carefully.

Foliage This should be clean, a deep color green, and not floppy and dehydrated.

Compost Examine the surface to make sure that there are no dead roots showing, which indicates that the root system is not healthy.

Leaves Check the undersides for any bugs that may be hiding there.

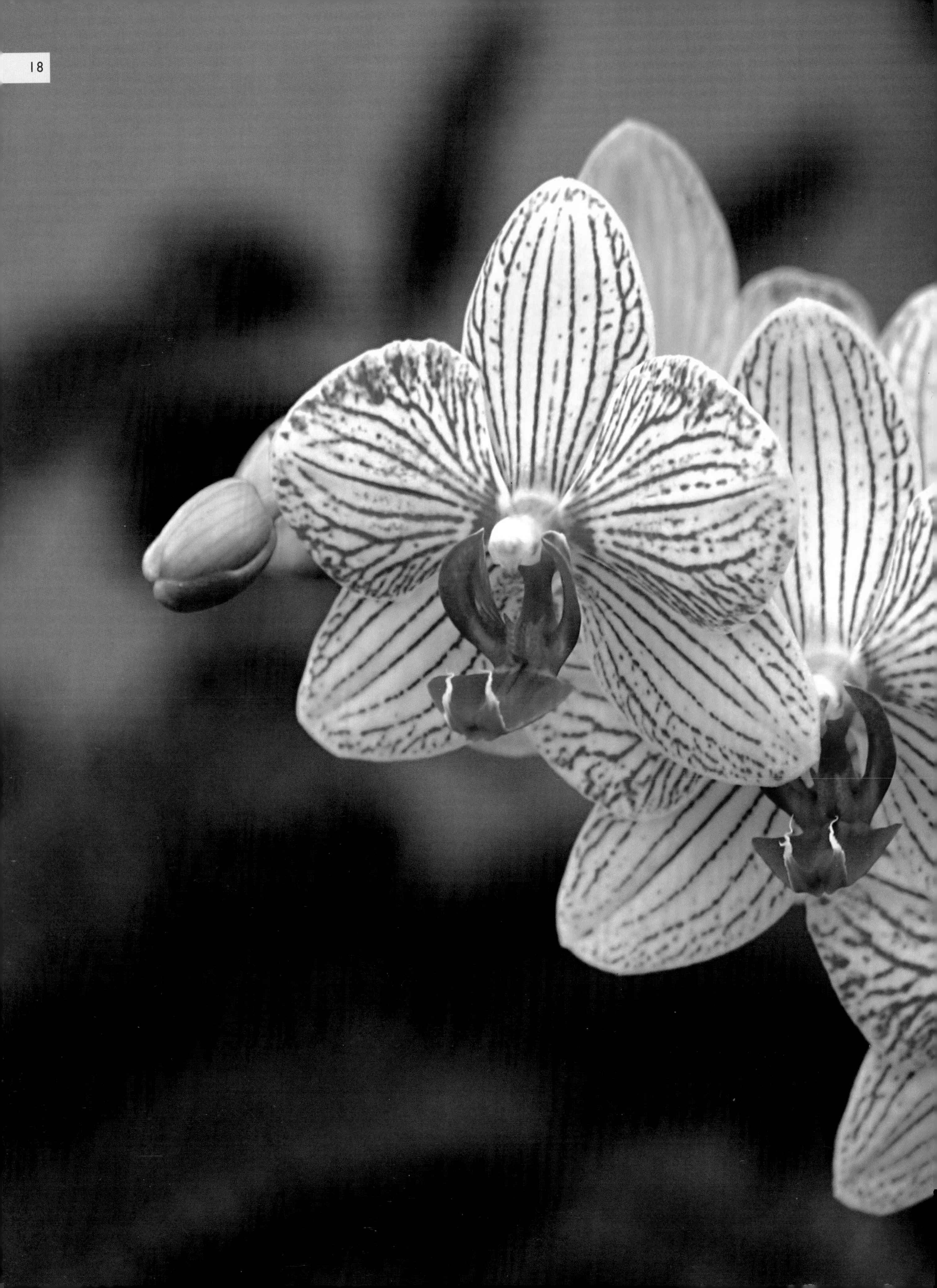

phalaenopsis

As popular as they are graceful, Moth Orchids can be grown in the home just about anywhere in the world. Phalaenopsis have no equal as a first orchid, since they are adaptable and tolerant of various climates. The blooms have wide, flat petals overlapping the sepals, with a small neat lip between them. Colors range from pristine white with either a yellow or red lip through buttery yellow to bright pink, with red-mauve being a relatively new breakthrough in the color spectrum. The petals can be plain or bedecked with spotting or candy stripes, adding to their allure, and the lips are always distinctively colored.

Phalaenopsis (Fal-en-op-sis)

Common name Moth Orchid. From the Greek, meaning "mothlike." Genus established in 1825. About 46 species, mostly from the Philippines and Indonesia.

all about phalaenopsis

Phalaenopsis bloom for the first time when they are four to five years old, but once they have flowered, they can bloom two or three times in a year. The buds at the lower end of the flower spike open first, and the blooms can last for months.

Phalaenopsis can tolerate a short time in dappled sunlight, but never stand them in direct sun.

Phalaenopsis are compact growing plants with a few rounded oval leaves that grow in a left-right formation from a central rhizome, or underground stem. The mid- to dark-green leaves are fairly rigid, so they can snap easily if handled roughly. The plants can live for many years, continuing to produce new leaves while periodically losing the oldest ones from the base. Because of this, the plants never become too large; they stay roughly the same size throughout their lives.

Around the base of the plant are the thick, silvery aerial roots, which are different from the roots inside the pot. When the aerial roots are active you will see green tips growing at the ends. As these extend, the roots become covered in a silvery white, moisture-absorbing covering. This is why you need to mist the roots lightly every time you water. The aerial roots are extremely brittle and can be easily damaged, so be careful, especially with the tip.

Look for the developing flower spike at the base of the plant, inside the leaf axil. At first you will see what looks like a small green knob, not unlike a new root. As it starts to grow upward, it becomes more easily recognizable and before long the buds will show at the top. Over the next few weeks the buds spread out and swell to their eventual size before opening, one or two at a time, until the whole flower spike is in bloom.

GROWING WILD

Today's exquisite hybrids have been bred over many generations from the species, which are the naturally occurring wild plants. They originated in the humid tropical jungle of the Philippines, Borneo, and Indonesia. Here, they thrive on the branches of forest trees, an ideal existence in a warm climate. With little variation between the seasons, apart from the amount of rainfall, and shaded from the bright sun by the leaf canopy, phalaenopsis were completely in harmony with their surroundings. Their long flower spikes drooped from the branches and their flowers shimmered in the breeze, creating an effect of moths dancing on the wind. When seen from the ground, this is how they appeared to the first orchid hunters, and this is how they got the common name of Moth Orchid.

High among the branches in a wildlife sanctuary in East Thailand, phalaenopsis still flourish in the steamy warmth and dappled light.

HELPFUL HINTS

SITE
Warm room indoors,
away from direct sun.

OUTDOORS OR IN?
Do not put outdoors,
even in summer.

CARE
Keep watered all year
round, but do not
overwater.

WHEN TO REPOT
Repot every few years
after flowering, but
avoid disturbing the
plant during mid-
winter.

SIZE
Adult plants can reach
45 inches (112 cm) in
height, with blooms up
to 3 inches (7 cm)
across.

caring for moth orchids

Phalaenopsis will thrive indoors if you provide them with warmth and humidity and keep them evenly moist and out of direct sunlight.

Healthy phalaenopsis should have firm, semi-erect leaves. If they become soft or wrinkled, the most likely cause is overwatering, since the roots will die in saturated compost. Without the roots to take up moisture, the leaves will get dehydrated and become limp. The same thing will happen when a plant has been underwatered and the roots cannot find enough moisture in the pot. The remedy for the overwatered plant is to repot it immediately. If it is in bloom, cut off the flower spike; the flowers will last a while if placed in water. You may have to wait several weeks before new roots start to grow, and only then will the plant start to recover. During this time lightly spray the foliage to prevent any further moisture loss, but do not water.

For the underwatered plant, start by giving it a good soak for up to five minutes in a bowl of water and allowing it to drain. Avoid getting water into the center of the plant, since this can cause it to rot. If rot develops, the plant may start to grow again from the base, but a few years will pass before it will bloom again.

Phalaenopsis can withstand a wide range in temperature—up to 80°F (27°C) in summer and down to 64°F (18°C) on winter nights—but they will suffer from heat stress or cold when it is hotter or colder than the recommended temperatures. Plants that have been exposed to extreme cold will have limp, semi-transparent foliage; those suffering from overheating will simply become limp due to dehydration. They may recover if given improved conditions in a position that suits them better.

Always keep phalaenopsis out of direct sunlight, which can cause scorching; this will show up as an ugly dark patch on the leaf. Once the plant has been moved to a better position, the burn will not go away, but it will not get any worse.

Bud blast

Where conditions are not quite right, it is common for the long-awaited buds to turn yellow and drop off just as they were about to open. Bud blast most often occurs during the winter months when there is little light, or when conditions are cold and damp. Moving the plant to a better position in the room will often stop this from happening again. Cut the flower spike back to a lower leaf node and the next buds may develop normally.

If after some weeks the plant does not show any improvement in the new location, you may have to look for another cause. The plant may be suffering from dryness in the pot or surroundings. Buds, being the softest part of the plant, are susceptible to conditions in the environment that may not affect the plant itself.

Encouraging a new flower spike

As the flowers come to the end of their life, they turn papery before dropping off, but with phalaenopsis you can expect a bonus. At intervals

Gently wipe the leaves with a damp cloth to remove any dust that has settled on them.

along the flower spike, there are several nodes, each covered by a small green, leaflike sheath. Cut the top part of the flower spike between two of the lower nodes to activate a second branch of flowers; another branch will form almost every time. After you have enjoyed this second blooming, you will need to cut the flower spike down to within about 1 inch (2.5 cm) of the base. Before

long the plant will make a new flower spike. In the meantime, your phalaenopsis will probably also produce a new leaf, a sure sign of health.

Phalaenopsis are not seasonal orchids. They bloom at any time and can often provide two or three flowering spikes in a year. An older, mature plant may remain in bloom for several years with hardly a pause, one flower spike following another in a continual succession.

When a flower spike has grown to 6 inches (15 cm), place a split bamboo cane in the compost close to it and tie it in just below the buds so that the spike extends and arches over naturally.

DO'S

✓ Water throughout the year and feed at every second or third watering.

✓ Grow in the shade on a north-facing windowsill or in the center of a room.

✓ Repot occasionally after flowering to remove old, decaying compost.

✓ Tie the flower spike to a cane when the plant is in bloom so that the heavy flowers do not pull the spike over.

DON'TS

✗ Do not grow in full sun.

✗ Do not spray the leaves too heavily; water lodging in the crown can cause rot.

✗ Do not allow to get too cold—below 64°F (18°C) on a winter's night.

✗ Do not allow to get too hot—over 80°F (27°C).

✗ Do not divide the plant when repotting.

MEALYBUGS

The most likely pests to affect phalaenopsis are mealybugs (see p.180). They can be seen on any part of the plant, often hiding under the leaves or around the rim of the pot. They seem to move to new feeding areas at night, so check the plants daily if you suspect they are present. They damage the plant by sucking sap from the leaves, which can lead to further infection. The easiest way to eradicate the pests is to dab each one with a cotton swab or paintbrush dipped in rubbing alcohol. This kills the pests immediately.

repotting moth orchids

Your Phalaenopsis plant requires the least attention of all orchids when it comes to repotting, and the plant should not need to be repotted for several years after you buy it.

You need to repot your phalaenopsis when a number of dead roots can be seen on the surface of the compost and the condition of the compost is so poor that you can push your finger through it. Since phalaenopsis grow steadily throughout the year and are often in bloom, you will need to pick a time to repot when the plant has finished flowering. You should avoid disturbing it during the coldest months of the year when the daylight hours are short. Plants repotted in mid-winter will take longer to recover and start growing again. Most plants can be repotted in the same size pot or one only slightly larger. Do not be tempted to use a pot that is too large, since that can lead to overwatering—with dire consequences. A newly repotted plant will need less frequent watering than one that has become pot-bound. When repotting, you will need plenty of space to work and some old newspapers to work on.

Phalaenopsis do not readily propagate; only very occasionally will a new plantlet form on a mature flower spike. Where this occurs, a plantlet grows instead of flowers. Leave the new plant until it has made its own roots. You can then cut it off and pot it independently.

REPOTTING A PHALAENOPSIS

YOU WILL NEED:
◆ Compost, either natural (fir bark chips, medium grade) or synthetic (Rockwool or Stonewool)
◆ Old newspapers
◆ Craft knife or pruning shears
◆ Polystyrene chips or other drainage material
◆ New pot
◆ Protective gloves and mask, if using synthetic compost

1

A plant needs repotting when dry, dead roots show on the surface of the compost. If you check the compost, you will probably find it full of dead roots as well. The plant will also be unable to support new root growth.

Remove the plant from its pot, shake out the old compost and gently tease it out from between the roots.

2

Keep the air moist by standing the plants on a bed of pebbles placed at the bottom of a large container and adding water to just reach the top of the pebbles.

3

Cut back any dead roots and trim the live ones with a pair of pruning shears or a sharp craft knife.

Place the plant in the center of the pot with its aerial roots above the compost. Pack the compost around the plant so that it is firm and upright.

4

5

A well-potted plant will soon start to grow again. It will produce new leaves and roots and a flower spike with several developing buds.

◀ *Phalaenopsis* Brother Wild Thing

The basic color of this flower is white, overlaid with a
pattern of deep pink spotting. It has a pink lip. Today, many
beautiful phalaenopsis are being bred all over the world.
This variety from Taiwan represents a new breed of
spotted and patterned flowers.

Phalaenopsis Hawaiian Darling ▲

A delicate hint of pink suffuses the white flowers of this
orchid, making the contrasting cherry red lip stand out
boldly. The semi-arching spikes are the perfect decoration
for the house or office, and the blooms will last for
months in perfect condition.

Phalaenopsis Sonata Spots ▶

Fascinating, irregular crimson markings dapple the white background on these flowers. The orange and red decorating the lips is known as Leopard Lips. Mature plants will often produce branching spikes, a legacy from the species from which this hybrid has been bred. This orchid is another variety from Taiwan.

Phalaenopsis Purple Valley ▼

This is a notable deep rose-pink phalaenopsis with a darker lip. These dark colors do not exist in the species and can be produced only by selective breeding. They are among the most popular colors, second only to white.

SITE
Warm room indoors, away from direct sun.

OUTDOORS OR IN?
Do not put outdoors, even in summer.

CARE
Keep watered all year round, but do not overwater.

WHEN TO REPOT
Repot every few years after flowering, but avoid disturbing the plant during the shortest days of winter.

SIZE
Adult plants are 9 inches (23 cm) high and across. Blooms are 3 inches (7 cm) or more across.

◀ *Phalaenopsis* Miva Re Chopin

The attractive peach-pink petals of this orchid are patterned with stripes and veining, while the large lip is maroon and gold. This French hybrid represents a breeding line of coffee table Moth Orchid, so called because they are small enough to use for table decoration. They have proved popular because of their compact growth and unusual coloring.

Phalaenopsis Barbara Moler x *P. Mannii* ▶

This orchid is a recent cross using the species *P. mannii*, which is responsible for the red and yellow, rather pointed petals and sepals. This gives the plant a character all of its own. The shape of the flower is different from the more common rounded flower shape usually associated with phalaenopsis that resulted from crossing orchids several generations removed from the species plants.

◀ *Phalaenopsis* Happy Girl

Most phalaenopsis have different color lips and petals. Some lips are yellow, orange, or pink, but the most startling combinations occur with the cherry reds. Here, the cherry red lip is in striking contrast to the pristine white petals. This plant has the same long-lasting qualities as all the other white-flowered phalaenopsis.

Phalaenopsis Petite Snow ▶

This compact plant has branching spikes that bear many small, rosy pink flowers with a gold and maroon lip. The dominant species is *P. equestris*. When this has been hybridized with other colors, such as whites, pinks, and yellows, a new range of miniature phalaenopsis has emerged.

Phalaenopsis Danielle ▶

This lemon yellow orchid has faint red striping on the petals and sepals. The lip is a darker red with some gold markings. When the flower first opens, the color is very rich; it gradually tones to a lighter shade. The flowers will hold their color longer if kept out of strong light.

Phalaenopsis Dragon's Charm ▲

A beautiful nonfading, chrome yellow flower, lightly peppered with red, and a gold and red lip distinguish this orchid. A few years ago, such high-quality yellows were unobtainable, but modern breeding has achieved outstanding results. At present, the number of flowers produced per spike is limited, but the aim of breeders is to increase the number of flowers in the future.

◄ *Phalaenopsis* Falre Spots

The petals and sepals here are so heavily marked with dramatic crimson that little of the white can be seen. The flower has an even darker lip and a pure white pollen cap in the center. This beautiful and unusual bloom is the very latest in modern breeding.

Phalaenopsis Gojonat ▼

The pastel pink flowers have a dark lip, and the back of the petals is often a darker shade of pink than the front. By interbreeding the pink orchids with the large red lipped whites, a pale pink with high-quality flowers has been produced.

▼ *Phalaenopsis* Yellow Treasure

Solid bright yellow petals, sepals suffused with pink in the center, and a lemon lip make this a remarkable orchid. Yellows of this quality are greatly sought after by collectors of unusual phalaenopsis. Although the number of flowers is limited, the plant can produce several flower spikes at one time.

◄ *Phalaenopsis* Sweet Memory

The petite sunset red flowers, paler at the tips, are achieved from the same breeding lines as the yellows, but only the darker shades are selected. Breeders hope to achieve even more intense reds with more blooms per flower spike in the future.

Phalaenopsis Orchid World ▶

This is a much advanced hybrid from the original species *P. amboinensis* and *P. violacea.* The base color of yellow with a hint of green has a pattern of maroon bars and stripes radiating like a cobweb from the center of the flower. As a result of its parentage, this orchid tends to have only two or three flowers open at one time.

◀ *Phalaenopsis* Malibou Mystere

These large, pure white flowers, with a touch of gold on the lip, have the texture of high-quality art paper. All whites originate from a single species, *P. amabilis,* and were the earliest phalaenopsis to be hybridized; consequently, they bear little resemblance to the original species. Their flowers are larger and longer lasting than those of any other phalaenopsis.

cymbidiums

Cymbidiums certainly let you know they are there! The plants are tall, with graceful foliage, and the blooms are large and waxy, with petals, sepals, and lip all equal in size. The staggering color range covers virtually every shade except blue. The blooms are usually plain, but you can find an occasional flower with some striping or spotting. The lip is mostly white, boldly marked around the margin with yellow or various shades of red. This color combination gives rise to fantastic contrasts, such as refreshing apple green or intense yellow petals and sepals with a bright red-margined lip. Pure white, with little lip adornment, is a further delight, while at the other end of the color range there are brooding mahogany red and bronze shades, all part of the rich tapestry of color that cymbidiums display.

Cymbidium (Sim-bid-ee—um)

From the Greek, meaning "boat-shaped," referring to the shape of the lip. Genus established in 1799. About 50 species from India and elsewhere in Asia. Most hybrids are produced from the Indian species.

all about cymbidiums

For more than 100 years, cymbidiums have been among the most popular orchids. At one time, it was not unusual for an amateur's collection to consist solely of many beautiful and varied cymbidium hybrids.

In the wild, many cymbidiums flourish as epiphytes high among the branches in mountain forests.

Many thousands of *Cymbidium* hybrids have been raised from just a handful of species, which originated in the Himalayas, where they grow either in the ground or upon trees. They flourish at high altitudes in mountainous terrain, where the nights are cool and there are monsoons for part of the year. In cultivation, they are able to grow in cooler parts of the world, where temperatures range from 50–86°F (10–30°C). Cymbidiums cannot tolerate too much heat, which can weaken the plant and cause stress, leading to disease.

Growing and flowering

Cymbidiums produce rounded pseudobulbs sheathed in the bases of the leaves. New pseudobulbs start as young growths that sprout from the base of the previous pseudobulb and continue to grow for nine months or so, before maturing with eight to ten leaves.

As a new pseudobulb matures, a flower spike will start to form at the base. At first it looks the same as the new growth, but within weeks the flower spike will look like a fat pencil, while the new growth quickly fans out into leaves. The newest pseudobulbs usually produce the flower spikes. As each pseudobulb ages, the leaves are shed over a one or two year period, until it becomes leafless. The leafless pseudobulb, now called a backbulb, will remain alive for a few more years, becoming a source of nourishment for the younger growth. Backbulbs are not dead until they become brown and shriveled; they can then be removed from the plant when you are repotting it.

Flower spikes can reach 3 feet (1 m) tall, and on a large plant you can expect up to six flower spikes in one season, each with a dozen or so stunning blooms up to 4 inches (10 cm) across. The blooms will last in perfect condition for six to eight weeks, and the plant may remain in bloom for much longer if several flower spikes open in succession. Once it has flowered, the pseudobulb will not produce a flower spike again.

Some *Cymbidium* hybrids have a slight fragrance, especially those with green flowers. This fragrance is most noticeable on bright, sunny mornings.

GROWING CYMBIDIUMS OUTDOORS

In warm regions, cymbidiums can be grown outdoors all year round in permanent beds made up of a loose compost. Here, they will grow to their full potential and are most impressive. Plant them in partial shade—to prevent the bright midday sun from burning the foliage—and be sure to water regularly and spray overhead.

In cooler climates, cymbidiums can be moved outdoors for the summer and brought inside again during the winter. Growing cymbidiums indoors all year can limit the amount of light they get, and this can have an effect on their flowering ability. The extra light they get outside will help them produce better blooms.

HELPFUL HINTS

SITE
Cool, well-lit area where the temperature drops to 50–55°F (10–13°C) at night and never rises above 86°F (30°C) in the daytime.

OUTDOORS OR IN?
Outdoors year-round in mild climates; only in summer in places with cold winters.

CARE
Keep watered all year. Add feed every second watering in summer; every third in winter.

WHEN TO REPOT
Repot after flowering, every two years.

SIZE
Adult plants can reach 3 feet (1 m) in height. Blooms are up to 4 inches (10 cm) across.

caring for cymbidiums

Given plenty of light and cool nights, coupled with year-round watering, cymbidiums will flourish, whether growing indoors or out.

Grow cymbidiums in a cool, well-lit area where the temperature drops at night to 50–55°F (10–13°C). In winter, an occasional drop to a few degrees below 50°F (10°C) will do no harm. Summer daytime temperatures should not go above 86°F (30°C). During hot summers, the best environment would be a cool, air-conditioned room where the light is good.

Cymbidium hybrids grow for most of the year without a definite rest period. You should water the plants all year to keep the pseudobulbs plump, adding feed to the water at every second watering in summer but only at every third watering in winter. Keep the plants slightly drier in winter, when their growth is slower.

These orchids have a thick rooting system. New roots form from new growths as they develop. In time, the roots will completely fill the container, often pushing the plant up above the rim. This makes watering difficult, since most of the water poured over the surface runs off without penetrating the root ball. As the older pseudobulbs mature and become leafless, their roots will die.

Flowering

Cymbidium flower spikes start to emerge from early summer onward. Support them as they extend to keep them from bending over and even snapping under their own weight. Insert a bamboo cane as close as possible to the flower spike, but away from the rim of the pot where most of the

Stake the flower spikes of cymbidiums so that the heavy blooms do not break the flower spike with their weight.

DO'S

✔ Tie the flower spike to a cane so that the heavy flowers do not pull the spike over and break it.

✔ Water regularly throughout the year. Feed at every second watering in summer, every third in winter. Spray overhead.

✔ Grow in semi-shade outdoors; in the house grow in cool conditions, with plenty of light.

✔ Repot every two years, after flowering.

✔ Divide the plant when repotting if it has formed two separate sections.

DON'TS

✘ Do not grow in full sun.

✘ Do not allow to get too cold—below 50°F (10°C) on a winter's night.

✘ Do not allow to get too hot—over 86°F (30°C) in summer.

roots are. Use one or two loose ties around the spike and cane.

As the flower spike lengthens, you will see small buds emerging from the top. Place the last tie at the base of the buds so that the top portion can develop freely. Later, when the flower spike has stopped growing and the buds have all opened out, it may be necessary to place another tie between the opened buds to keep the flowers upright. If the cane you are using is longer than the top buds, cut it off with gardening shears in order to avoid any accidental injury to anyone admiring the plant.

Care for the leaves by wiping them frequently

Cymbidiums in flower look glorious against a background of green foliage.

To check for red spider mites, wipe the leaves with a white cloth or tissue: the minute, pale orange mites can be more easily seen against the white surface.

with plain water so that they remain clean and free from dust. Do not use leaf shine, since this tends to clog the pores and the leaves cannot breathe.

The leaves can live for several years and may become cracked or broken, or marked with age. Cut off any damaged leaves and trim back any black tips to keep the plant looking its best. Older leaves turn yellow naturally and can be left until they drop and then you can remove them.

Premature loss of foliage occurs when a number of the leaves turn yellow at the same time. The main causes are exposure to cold or overwatering. Once a plant has lost all or most of its foliage so dramatically, you probably cannot save it; the road back to good health could be a long one.

The most common pest to attack cymbidiums is red spider mites (see p. 180). These are extremely small but harmful sap-sucking pests. Use a magnifying glass to observe the undersides of the leaves where they cause silvery patches; later, these patches will turn black if a secondary infestation contaminates the leaves.

44

repotting cymbidiums

*Cymbidiums need to be repotted when the roots
have lifted the plant over the edge of the pot,
or the leading pseudobulb has reached the rim.*

Cymbidiums will stay healthier and flower better if
they are repotted every two years. If a plant has
not been repotted for many years, the center will
contain dead parts, while all the new growth will
be crowded around the rim or over the edge of
the pot. Repotting at this stage may cause severe
shock because so much will have to be cut away.
It can take a few years for the plant to recover fully
and flower again.

The best time to repot is when all the flowers
have withered and the last flower spike is cut back.
Once the oldest blooms start to fade, cut each
flower spike down to within 1 inch (2.5 cm) of the
base and take out the cane supporting it. Stop
watering the plant a few days before you repot it
so that it can dry out.

During repotting you will clean out the dead
roots and backbulbs and give the plant a fresh start
in new compost. Be sure there is sufficient room at
the front of the pot for the plant to grow forward.
The pot should be large enough for another two
years of growing; one the next size up should work
well. If you use a pot that is too large, you may
overwater, which will cause the roots to rot.

Dividing a large plant

Cymbidiums can live for many years, growing bigger
all the time. To maintain them at a manageable size,
divide plants about every four years. When dividing,
leave at least four pseudobulbs and make sure that
there is a new growth on each part of the plant.
A plant divided smaller than this will not flower
until sufficient pseudobulbs have built up again.

REPOTTING A CYMBIDIUM

YOU WILL NEED:

◆ Compost, either natural (fir
bark chips, medium grade) or
synthetic (Rockwool)
◆ Old newspapers
◆ Craft knife or pruning
shears
◆ Polystyrene chips or other
drainage material
◆ New pot
◆ Protective gloves and mask,
if using Rockwool

**Take the plant out
of its pot** and examine
the roots. Old roots are
brown, new roots white.

The plant should look like the
plant on the left after the roots
have been trimmed.

Cut out any dry, dead roots. Trim back the live ones on each part of the plant to about 6 inches (15 cm).

3

2

Tease apart the roots. If the plant has formed two sections, separate them by cutting through the rhizome between the pseudobulbs with a sharp knife.

Hold the plant so that the base of the pseudobulbs is just below the rim of the pot. The leading growth must be level with the compost surface. Pack in the compost with your other hand. Wait for a few days before watering.

6

5

Choose the right size pot to allow for 2 years' forward growth. Add material such as polystyrene chips to aid drainage.

▼ *Cymbidium* Rossignol

The classic, deep pink coloring—a color for all seasons—
makes this orchid an enduring favorite. Pink cymbidiums such
as this can be found throughout the whole *Cymbidium*
flowering season, from fall all the way through to late spring.

Cymbidium Cristow ▶

The richness of this flower is clearly seen in
the deep rosy pink coloring, which borders on
red. Even after the blooms have been open
for many weeks, they will still keep their color.
The lip coloring is much darker—almost black
by comparison. Heavy flower spikes like this
need some support as they grow to stop
them from snapping under their own weight.

▼ *Cymbidium* Summer Pearl

This delightful miniature variety blooms during the summer—a tribute to the hybridizer's skill. The blooms are ivory-white, toning to a clouded white as they age. The neat lips are generously adorned with red markings. The flowers have a slight fragrance inherited from the original species, although this hybrid is several generations removed.

Cymbidium Happy Days ▶

A delicate scent hangs over this ice green standard hybrid. It is a color that suits all tastes because its endearing qualities give a fresh, cool look to any dull corner. The lip is lightly spotted with pale red. This plant should bloom in early spring.

Cymbidium Ming ▶

A miniature hybrid, this delightful winter-blooming orchid carries numerous flowers on an upright flower spike. The chrome yellow sepals and petals have a faint red stripe at their center. The white lip is richly decorated with mahogany red. This free-flowering variety will bloom for many weeks.

◀ Cymbidium Mini Mint

This little charmer is a miniature clone, bred to be small and compact. It is suitable for growing indoors where space is limited. Extremely free-flowering, it will produce several flower spikes on a comparatively small plant. The clear, lime green coloring of the sepals and petals makes a pleasing contrast with the cream-colored, yellow-dotted lip.

◀ *Cymbidium* Archirondel

This superb, modern standard hybrid exhibits the classic *Cymbidium* flower shape, with generously wide petals and sepals that are slightly cupped when fully open. The pale, off-white coloring contrasts strongly with the dark red lip decoration, which is echoed in the slight peppering at the base of the sepals.

Cymbidium Cotil Point ▶

The flower spikes of this full-petaled, standard hybrid can be trained upright or allowed to arch. The large, deep rosy-pink flowers are decorated with rounded lips that carry a distinctive red margin that emphasizes the beauty of this lovely clone.

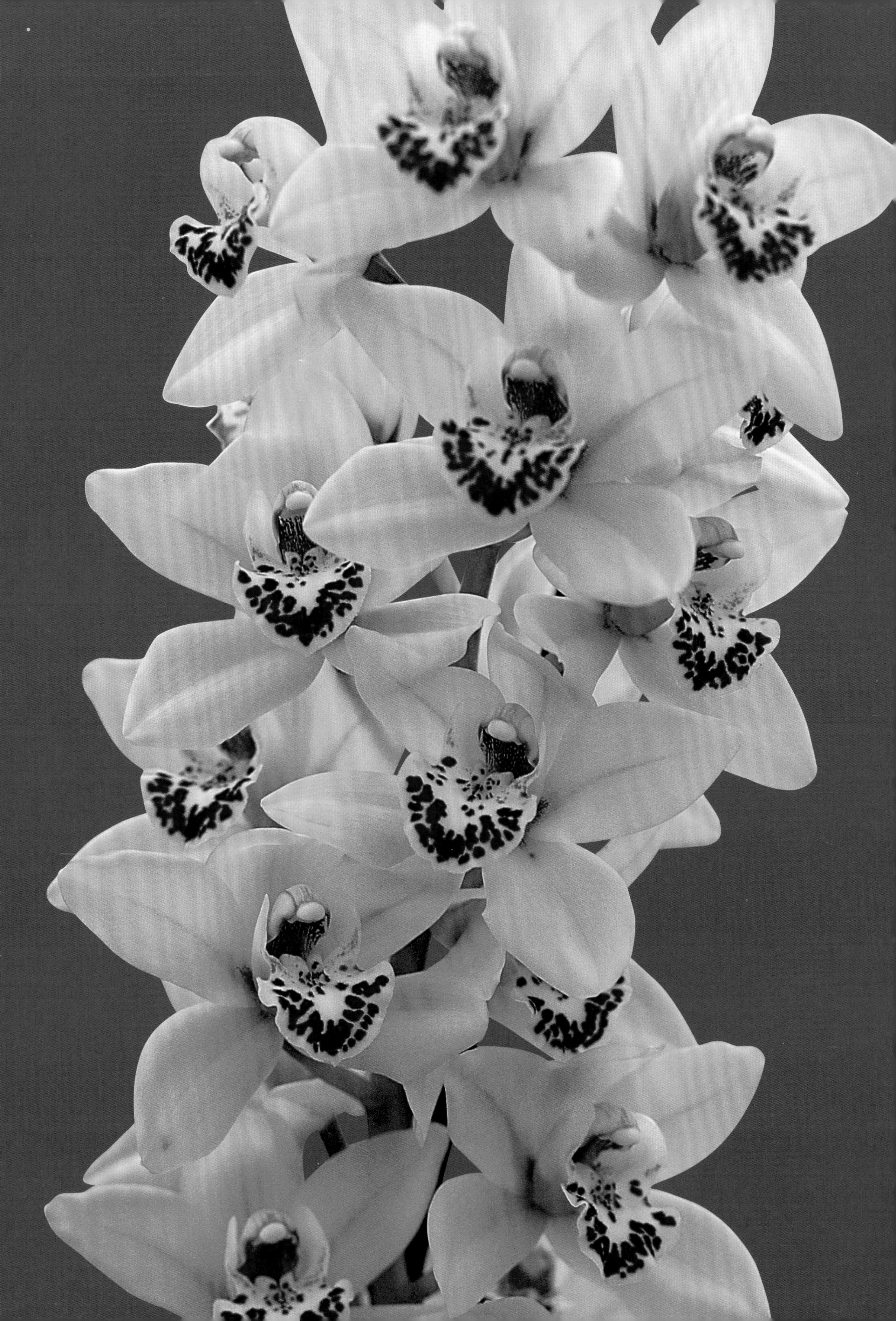

◄ *Cymbidium* Via Vista

An extremely attractive compact hybrid, this plant's blooms are smaller than those of the standard types. They are seen at their best if trained upright, so that they stand well above the foliage. The flowers are a soft creamy yellow, enhanced by the dark red, horseshoe-shaped decoration on the lip.

▼ *Cymbidium* Pontac

Cymbidiums do not come much redder than this richly colored variety, guaranteed to brighten the dullest of winter days. In sunny climates, keep the flowers out of direct sunlight so that they hold their color and do not fade. This hybrid does not produce many blooms on a flower spike, but the blooms that appear are fairly large.

▲ *Cymbidium* Samarkand 'Top Flight'

A long-time favorite, this hybrid has classic old-gold hues that are always in demand. It is well loved by growers throughout the world. Typical of many varieties in its species that are always available, this hybrid will never lose its allure or its ability to delight when in bloom.

◀ *Cymbidium* Saint Helier 'Mont Millias'

This outstanding clone was given an Award of Merit by the Royal Horticultural Society in London for its excellent shape and quality. It blooms in early summer, at the end of the main flowering season for cymbidiums. The frosty ice green of the petals and sepals matches the pale, unmarked lip.

◀ *Cymbidium* Nandy 'Green Mist'

One of the most popular of the standard green-flowered clones, this late-flowering specimen needs space to grow, since it can become quite large within a few years. The flower spikes carry a good number of large blooms in apple green, with china white lips that bear the distinctive red marking around the margin.

Cymbidium Avranches ▶

A gorgeous, deep sunshine-yellow glow is given off by this desirable standard hybrid. The yellow lip is adorned with dark red, providing a sparkling color combination. Deep yellows, such as this clone displays, are not often seen, but are well worth looking out for, since they positively shine.

the odontoglossum alliance

Once described as the Queen of Orchids, today odontoglossums are simply part of the *Odontoglossum* Alliance, which encompasses a group of related orchids that will readily interbreed. Cross-breeding odontoglossums with orchid genera such as *Cochlioda* and *Oncidium* has given rise to numerous hybrids. The result is a never-ending range of delightful blooms with patterns and frills galore. All colors are present except for the elusive blue, but blue-mauve tones are not uncommon. Some of the most vibrant colors are the bright sunshine yellows and deep sunset reds. Speckles and spots and heavy markings are the hallmarks of these orchids. Odontoglossums—and many of the orchids related to them—come from South America, where they grow on trees, high in the Andean cloud forest. They thrive in a cool, airy environment, where nights are often cold enough for frost, so in cultivation they do best in cooler regions.

Odontoglossum (O-<u>dont</u>-o-glos-um)

Common name: Queen of Orchids. From the Greek, meaning "tooth tongue," referring to the toothlike projections on the lip. Genus established in 1815. Sixty species from the Andes mountain range.

all about odontoglossums

Pure odontoglossums are now far less common than the intergeneric hybrids, which all come under the general heading of odontoglossums. Prized for their highly decorative flowers and easy to grow in the home, these hybrids are immensely popular.

Tall and elegant, this *Odontoglossum* hybrid, *Colmanara* Wild Cat 'Bobcat', produces a display of flowers that lasts for weeks. The tall flower spike will need support.

There is great variation in the flowers of *Odontoglossum* intergeneric hybrids, but they all conform to a basic shape, with sepals and petals of equal size and a distinctive lip that is larger than the rest of the flower in *Oncidium* hybrids and smaller in other hybrids. The flowers will last for up to six weeks and a plant will normally bloom once in its season (every nine to ten months). This means that the plant may bloom at a different time each year.

Odontoglossum types produce green, shiny, oval-shaped pseudobulbs with a pair of leaves at the apex, and two smaller leaves at the base. The flower spike comes from inside a basal leaf as the pseudobulb matures. The plants are compact, mostly less than 18 inches (45 cm) high, although on some the flower spikes can reach 3 feet (1 m).

As the new growths appear from the base of the pseudobulb, new roots are also produced. They are finer than those of other orchids and can grow until they completely fill the pot to become a tight ball of white growing roots. In time, the oldest pseudobulbs will lose their leaves, but will remain green and plump for a few more years to support the younger growths. As the old pseudobulbs die, they turn brown and can be cut away. Wait until you repot the plant, then cut away the old pseudobulbs if their roots are dead. The live roots will come from the newer pseudobulbs.

Intergeneric hybrids

One of the genera crossed with odontoglossums is *Cochlioda*, making *Odontioda*. The earliest hybrids were raised using red-flowered *Cochlioda noezliana*, which produced a vigorous, richly colored hybrid. Other crossings mixed the colors even further, reaching the ultimate in *Vuylstekeara* (see below).

Another popular hybrid is *Odontocidium*, which combines *Odontoglossum* with *Oncidium*. Some of the hybrids excel in their long, many-flowered, occasionally fragrant, willowy flower spikes with exquisite blooms in a wonderfully vibrant color range. Further variations occur where one genus has become dominant, stamping its influence on the characteristics of the flowers.

THE ULTIMATE HYBRID: VUYLSTEKEARA

Named for the Belgian grower who first crossed the genera, this hybrid has *Cochlioda*, *Miltonia*, and *Odontoglossum* parentage. The celebrated *Vuylstekeara* Cambria 'Plush' was awarded a First Class Certificate by Britain's Royal Horticultural Society in 1967 and the American Orchid Society in 1973 (see photo, p. 70). It has been more widely mass-produced than any other orchid—so much so, that today a multitude of similar odontoglossums are sold simply as "Cambria Orchids."

The large, boldly colored, deep wine red flowers show their *Miltonia* background, which has also influenced the large, fanned-out lip. The little *Cochlioda* is such a distant ancestor that its genetic contribution can be seen only on the list of parents, where it lives on in name alone.

HELPFUL HINTS

SITE
Windowsill in medium light, but no direct sun. Nighttime minimum of 50°F (10°C), maximum daytime temperature of 75°F (24°C).

OUTDOORS OR IN?
Never put outdoors, even in summer.

CARE
Keep evenly moist and apply fertilizer all year round. Provide high humidity.

WHEN TO REPOT
Repot after flowering, every two years.

SIZE
Most adult plants are less than 18 inches (45 cm) high, but flower spikes can reach 3 feet (1 m).

caring for odontoglossums

Extensive hybridizing among the orchids of the Odontoglossum Alliance has produced some extremely vigorous plants, making them among the easiest orchids to grow in a cool climate.

Odontoglossums like a position on a windowsill where they will receive light but no direct sunlight. In winter, the temperature should drop to, but never fall below, 50°F (10°C) for several hours on most nights. In summer, nighttime temperatures should drop to, but not below, 55°F (13°C). Daytime temperatures above 75°F (24°C) will cause heat stress and stop the plants from growing and flowering. Keep the maximum summer temperatures under control by making sure there is plenty of fresh air moving around the plants.

Once the flowers have finished, cut the flower spike down to a few inches (centimeters) from the base of the pseudobulb.

The importance of correct watering

Most problems that occur with odontoglossums are due in some way to watering. Odontoglossums that are given too much water can start to rot at the base because their pseudobulbs are not very tough. If only one pseudobulb has rotted, cut

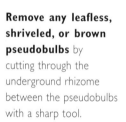

Remove any leafless, shriveled, or brown pseudobulbs by cutting through the underground rhizome between the pseudobulbs with a sharp tool.

through the rhizome immediately in front of this pseudobulb to prevent the rot from spreading to the rest of the plant (left).

Keep water away from the new growths, which are soft and lush and can rot at the base if water remains in the center. If the new growth turns brown, cut it off. Sometimes the plant will make another growth in place of the one you remove.

Incorrect watering—making the plant wet and dry in turn, instead of evenly moist—often causes the new leaves to become corrugated. Corrugation usually develops across the leaves but it can also occur along their length. Once this happens, little can be done, except to be more careful with watering in the future. If, however, despite careful watering, your plant always produces leaves with this problem, there may be a genetic fault. With so many plants being mass-produced, genetic faults can creep in and show up in this way.

Where winter temperatures remain too low for a long time, or where the temperature and humidity are not well balanced so that the plant gets cold and damp, water-filled blisters may occur on the pseudobulbs. The blisters can be popped open and drained. Dust the depressions with powdered sulfur so that the area dries up and does not become infected, causing more problems.

The main causes of shriveled pseudobulbs and spotting on leaves are overwatering or cold and damp. Poor conditions will weaken a plant, making it susceptible to fungal infection, which will attack the leaves. On older leaves, spotting may be no more than natural aging, but on new, young leaves it is an indication that growing conditions are not right. Black tips on the leaves are also a sign that conditions need to be improved.

The effect of light

In spring and early summer, direct sun on the plant will cause sunburn in the form of black patches on the leaves. Later in the summer, when light is at a maximum, a light reddish tinge may appear on the foliage. This is not harmful; it means that the plant is receiving the right amount of light. By winter, the foliage will return to mid-green.

If the leaves turn a deep reddish color in summer, they are receiving too much light. In extreme cases, this can cause premature leaf loss, which will result in more pseudobulbs being out of leaf than in leaf, and the plant will become unbalanced. To restore the balance, the leafless backbulbs must be removed. Take the plant out of its pot, cut off the surplus backbulbs, and repot the front section of the plant into a smaller pot. The plant will continue to grow forward and produce more good-sized pseudobulbs. Too many backbulbs will also cause the new pseudobulbs to be undersized, which may stop them from flowering.

Cleaning up the plant

When you repot the plant, clean it up by gently removing the old dead bases of the side leaves that surround the pseudobulbs. Cut off dead flower spikes, remove old canes, trim damaged leaves, and cut off black tips on old leaves.

WARM-GROWING RELATIONS

In tropical regions, odontoglossums do not do well, but a number of close relatives, including miltonias and hybrids bred from them, are far more tolerant of warmer climates (see Miltonias and Brassias, pp. 98–105).

WHEN TO REPOT

It is time to repot the plant when the new growth gets so close to the rim of the pot that inserting a finger between the plant and the pot is difficult (right).

You should repot the plant into a slightly larger container (see repotting cymbidiums pp.44–5), leaving room at the front of the plant for the new growth to develop (far right).

▼ *Wilsonara* Widecombe Fair

This intergeneric hybrid contains *Odontoglossum*, *Cochlioda,* and *Oncidium* in its pedigree. The most dominant of the three is the *Oncidium*, particularly the species *Oncidium incurvum*. This plant has given this lovely hybrid a tall, Christmas-tree type, branching flower spike. The individual blooms, in a combination of pink and white, are small and starry.

Miltonidium Avalon Bay ▶

In this crossing of *Miltonia* with *Oncidium*, the *Oncidium* has dominated and created a flower that is strikingly different, with its small, narrow petals and rich brown sepals. The lip is fiddle-shaped, large, and flared with a richly colored center and occasional spot at the base.

▲ *Odontoglossum* Augres

This classic white flower has an ageless appeal. Many hybrids can be found with the combination of pure white petals and sepals surrounding a distinctive yellow lip. Others in this same range show an occasional red or brown spot on the petals. Here, the lower part of the flower spike has been supported with a cane and the top flowers have been left to arch gracefully.

Odontoglossum Elle's Triumph ▶

Yellow odontoglossums are extremely popular, and this wonderful example of bright yellow and chestnut brown is hard to beat. The flowers show the classic patterning that represents the best to be found in this color range. With more buds still to open, this lovely clone will remain in bloom for many weeks.

Odontioda Kalkarstern ▶

This attractive orchid has been bred to produce slightly smaller flowers than is usual in these hybrids. The flower spike is shorter and lighter. The densely spotted petals and sepals are narrow and pointed, giving a star-shaped bloom. The heart-shaped lip is frilled, creating a pretty combination of cherry red and white.

◀ *Odontioda* Les Plantons

The fully mature flower spike on this orchid shows a plant in its prime. The large, expressive blooms have the delicate patterning typical of this lovely genus. While many plants exhibit similar coloring and markings, all are different, since each clone is an individual. Here, a white flower is almost totally suffused with a pink overlay and red spotting.

THE ODONTOGLOSSUM ALLIANCE   67

Odontioda Pontac ▶

Moving away from the rich colorings, this restful
flower is basically white, overlaid with delicate pink
and the occasional blotch of red. This is a young
plant blooming for the first time, so it is not carrying
a full-length flower spike (though it will on the next
flowering). When the orchid is mature, up to a dozen
blooms can be expected on the flower spike.

Oncidium Twinkle 'Red' ▼

Something completely different! This little charmer
has one species, *Oncidium ornithorhynchum,* in its
background that has created the modestly sized,
branching flower spikes with exquisitely shaped
pink blooms. As well as resembling the species
plant, the hybrid has inherited another attribute—
it is sweetly scented.

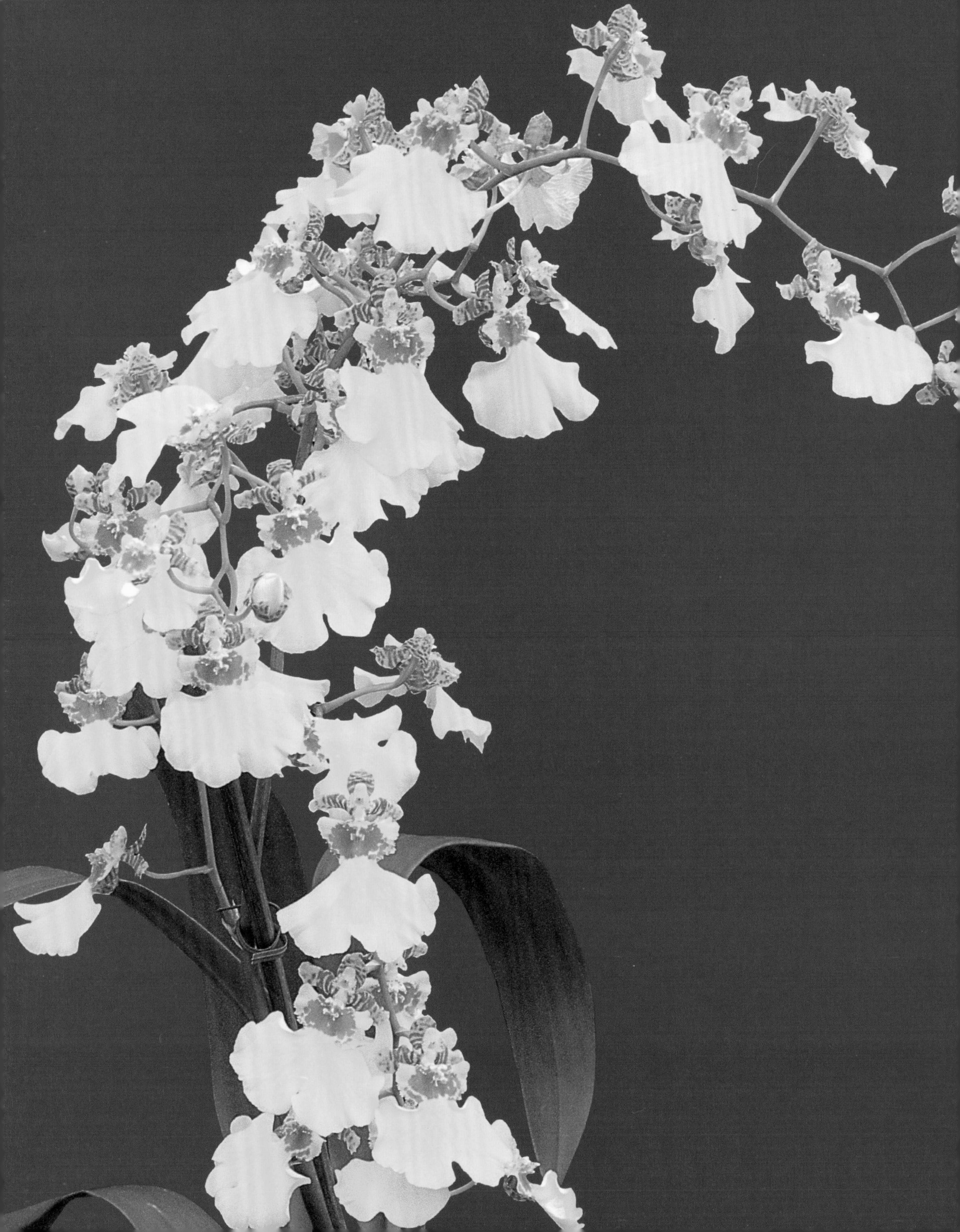

◀ *Oncidium* Boissiense

This striking hybrid is typical of large-lipped oncidiums that produce many flowered spikes of bright sunshine yellow. The petals and sepals are small, yellow spotted with red-brown, and partially hidden behind the round, flared lip that dominates the bloom. The flower spike branches, and the blooms are left to arch naturally.

▲ *Odontonia* Boussole 'Blanche'

This handsome bi-generic hybrid has been produced by combining *Odontoglossum* with *Miltonia*. The result is a large-flowered orchid with pointed petals and sepals of white suffused with pink; this coloring can be seen best on the outside of the flower. The flared lip is white and red patches surround the small yellow honey guide at the center.

◀ *Vuylstekeara* Cambria 'Plush'

This ageless classic is found wherever odontoglossums are grown. The tall flower spikes carry large, colorful blooms that are influenced by the *Miltonia* in the plant's background. This also accounts for the large, flamboyant lip, with its heavily spotted and peppered red outline. The petals and sepals are deep wine red.

Odontioda St. Clement ▶

Odontoglossum types produce patterns and colorings that are found in no other orchids to the same extent. This clone clearly illustrates the effect of a light base color overlaid with red-mauve blotches on the sepals and petals, which are rimmed with a similar color. The yellow stain at the center of the lip highlights the lovely coloring.

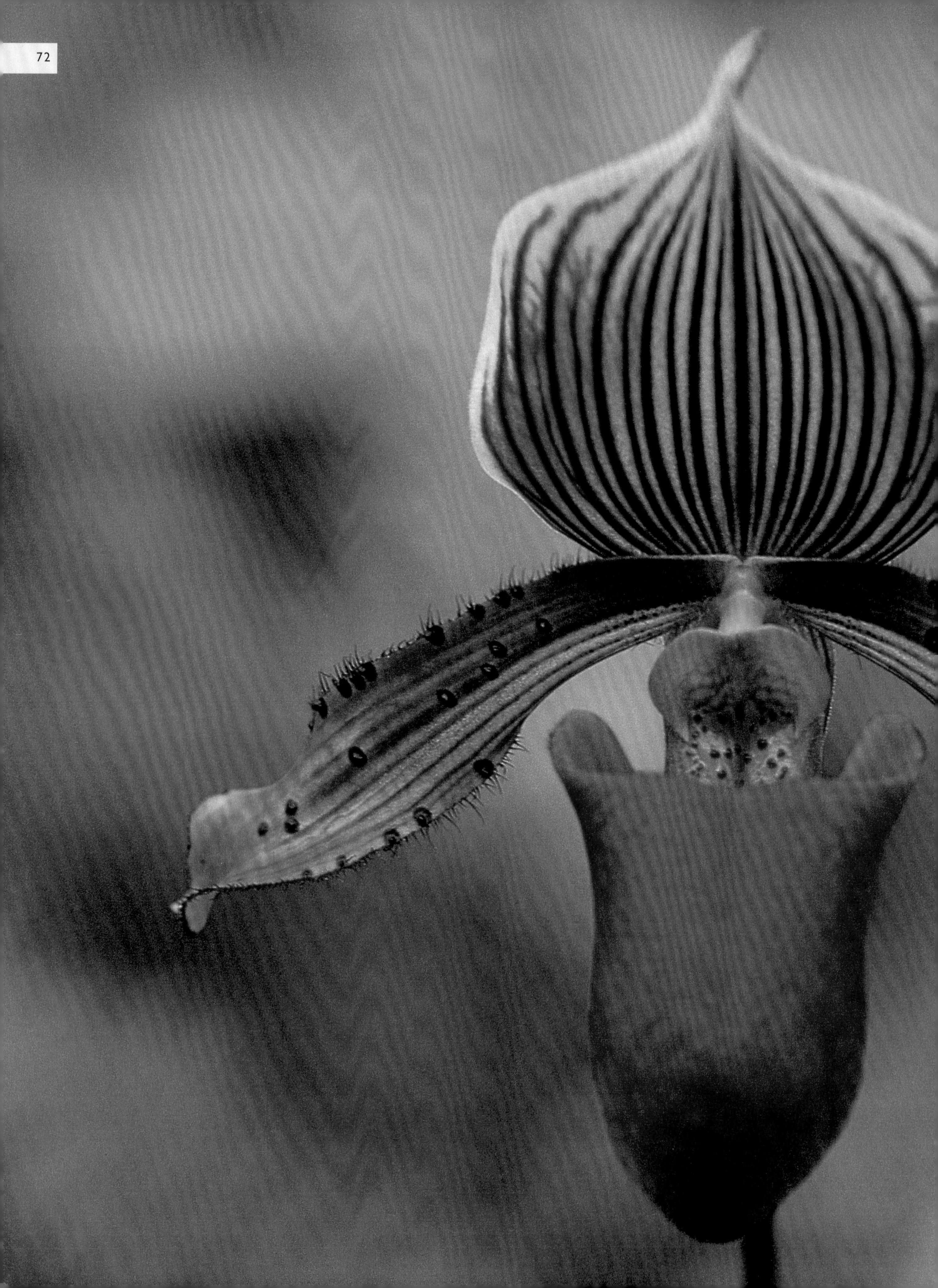

paphiopedilums and phragmipediums

These two handsome orchids, which come from different parts of the world, are both known as Slipper Orchids. They differ from other popular orchids mainly in the formation of the lip, which has become modified into a pouch that traps pollinating insects. When a bee tumbles into the pouch, it can exit only via a ladder of small hairs at the back of the pouch. As the bee crawls up to freedom, it dislodges the pollinia, or waxy clumps of pollen, which adhere to its body. The bee then carries the pollinia on to the next flower it visits. Above the pouch is the dorsal sepal and on either side are the petals. The two lateral sepals have become fused into one and are partially hidden behind the pouch.

Paphiopedilum (Paf-ee-oh-<u>ped</u>-i-lum)

Common name: Slipper Orchid. From the Greek, describing the lip shaped like Venus' slipper. Genus established in 1886. Sixty-five species from China to New Guinea. The species are rare, but many hybrids have been produced (see photo, left).

Phragmipedium (Frag-mi-<u>pee</u>-dee-um)

Common names: Slipper Orchid and Mandarin Orchid. From the Greek, meaning "divided shoe." Genus established in 1896. Twenty species known from South America. The number of hybrids has increased in recent years (see photo, p. 74).

all about slipper orchids

The flowers of both kinds of Slipper Orchid are similar, but paphiopedilums tend to be smaller and lower growing while phragmipediums have large leaves and longer flower spikes.

The dark red flowers appear in succession on this handsome *Phragmipedium*, so it will remain in bloom for months.

Both paphiopedilums and phragmipediums produce fleshy growths without pseudobulbs, which grow from a rhizome. Each new growth starts from the base of the previous one. Some plants produce few leaves, while others can have up to six.

Paphiopedilums

Many paphiopedilums are modest in size, with leaves just a few inches long, while others grow up to 12 inches (30 cm) high. The leaves can be very attractive, marbled or veined in light and dark green. There may be just one bloom on the spike or many, depending on the variety, and there is tremendous variation between the hybrids, which have been raised from many differing species.

The flowers can vary from 3 inches (7 cm) across the petals to those with 5-inch- (13-cm-) long petals, creating a flower more than 12 inches (30 cm) wide. The blooms can have a highly glossy appearance, with earthy brown and red, yellow and green, and white varieties. The flowers are often spotted, with decorative dorsal sepals that can be striped, flamed, or veined.

Each plant is an individual rather than a clone. Paphiopedilums must all be raised from seeds, since unlike many other orchids, mericloning does not work with them.

Phragmipediums

Phragmipediums are giants by comparison. They are robust and produce large, fleshy growths with leaves as long as 2 feet (60 cm). The flower spikes are tall, on some types extending eventually to 3 feet (1 m) or more; these types give a succession of blooms over many months. The fabled hybrid Mandarin Orchids produce large blooms with long, ribbonlike petals that droop to 6 inches (15 cm). Their colors range from tawny yellow through light green and brown to the turbulent orange and red-hot colors of the new hybrids.

GROWING WILD

Some species of paphiopedilums and phragmipediums grow in fallen leaves on the forest floor or in the lower branches of trees, while others grow on limestone outcrops or cling to sheer rock faces. They generally prefer fairly dry habitats that would not suit other orchids.

Paphiopedilum villosum in its natural habitat in Thailand.

PHRAGMIPEDIUM
(main picture)
HELPFUL HINTS

SITE
Warm room indoors with a minimum temperature of 55°F (13°C), away from direct sun.

OUTDOORS OR IN?
Never put outdoors, even in summer.

CARE
Keep watered all year round, but do not overwater. Wipe the leaves rather than spray the plant.

WHEN TO REPOT
Repot after flowering, every two years.

SIZE
Adult plants can grow to 3 feet (1 m) high. Blooms are up to 8 inches (20 cm) across.

PAPHIOPEDILUM
HELPFUL HINTS

SITE
Warm room indoors with a minimum temperature of 55°F (13°C), away from direct sun.

OUTDOORS OR IN?
Never put outdoors, even in summer.

CARE
Keep watered all year round, but do not overwater. Wipe the leaves rather than spray the plant.

WHEN TO REPOT
Repot after flowering, every two years.

SIZE
Adult plants are never more than about 12 inches (30 cm) high. Blooms can be up to 12 inches (30 cm) across.

caring for slipper orchids

Neither paphiopedilums nor phragmipediums have a definite resting or flowering period—they grow throughout the year.

As well as their common name, paphiopedilums and phragmipediums share many habits. They can be grown together in the same conditions—in warm to intermediate temperatures that do not drop below 55°F (13°C) on winter nights. Both need shade, but phragmipediums can take more light, provided that they are kept out of direct sun. During the winter, give both orchids as much light as possible indoors by putting them close to a sunny window. As spring advances and the days lengthen, move them to a spot where they will have more shade.

Given the right conditions, phragmipediums are vigorous growers. They need space to grow well and are best placed in a sunroom unless a greenhouse is available.

Paphiopedilums can be grown in compost consisting of bark chips, while phragmipediums do well in Rockwool. Rockwool retains a more constant moisture level around the roots, with less danger of rotting.

Watering and feeding

Since they grow and flower all year round, Slipper Orchids need constant watering. Try to keep them evenly moist, but never allow them to become too wet. If in doubt, always err on the dry side.

Apply feed directly to the pot as you water the plants. If they are dry, give plain water first and then the feed diluted in a second application of water. Applying fertilizer to very dry plants can have an adverse effect on the roots and may cause some

REVIVING A WATERLOGGED PAPHIOPEDILUM

Paphiopedilums that are consistently overwatered can lose their roots, or new roots can fail to grow. Such a plant will be loose in its pot, since there are no live roots to anchor it. A plant without roots will quickly become limp, and since a *Paphiopedilum* has no pseudobulbs, it will not have the reserves to withstand long periods of dehydration. Plants can sometimes be brought back to health by placing them in a sealed polyethylene bag or bottle with a little damp moss. Doing this will stop the dehydration, and if new growth is able to get started, new roots and recovery will follow.

Take the orchid out of its pot; cut a plastic bottle in half.

Place damp moss in the bottle and put the orchid in.

Cover with the top half of the bottle. Leave the cap off to allow air in.

burning. Phragmipediums growing in Rockwool can be fed at every watering, while paphiopedilums in compost should be fed only every second or third watering, depending on the time of the year—feed less in winter when light levels are lower and temperatures are cooler.

Do not spray these plants from overhead. Their leaves are susceptible to damp spots, which can be caused by too much water on the leaf. There is also the danger that sprayed water will run into the center of a growth, where it can cause rot to set in, with the loss of the whole growth. When you are watering the plant, be careful not to let any water splash into the growths.

Unlike those of other orchids, the old leaves remain on the plant long after they have died. It is best to cut them off at the base as they turn yellow. If you have to cut into any green part of the plant, always dust the severed edge with horticultural sulfur, particularly wherever damp spots occur.

Keep the air circulating

Fresh air is important to Slipper Orchids. Many obstacles to growing them successfully can be removed by increasing the air flow around the plants. Do not stand them close to a source of heat, such as a radiator or an appliance.

In summer, when temperatures are at, or near, their maximum, fresh air from an open window can be good for the plants. In winter, it becomes more difficult to give them fresh air without causing a draft, but try to find a situation where there is some movement of air. In a sunroom, you can keep the air circulating with a small electric fan. Air movement can also help to prevent problems caused by cold and damp or, at the other extreme, excessive heat.

Special problems

Look out for mealybugs (see p. 180), particularly on the undersides of the leaves, as well as in the center of the new growth. Mealybugs collecting here will attack the developing flower spike. They can often be found on the flower spike or on the flower itself once it opens.

Scale insects and red spider mites (see p. 180) will gain a hold where conditions are excessively warm and dry. The same conditions can cause black tips to appear on the leaves and premature yellowing of the foliage (see pp. 178–9).

With its elegant drooping petals, this paphiopedilum is a showstopper. It glows a deep wine red.

repotting slipper orchids

Paphiopedilums prefer organic compost,
such as fir bark chips, for planting, while
phragmipediums will thrive in Rockwool.

Paphiopedilums

Keeping the compost in good condition is vital for paphiopedilums. Once decomposed, compost does not let air circulate and becomes damp and sour. The plants will then quickly lose their roots. Repotting once a year stops this from happening. In spring, repot as you would a *Phragmipedium* (see below) but use fir bark and drainage material in the base. Do not repot if the plant is flowering.

Keep paphiopedilums in as small a pot as possible. Sometimes the pot may appear to be too small for the plant, but paphiopedilums have few roots compared to other orchids. Their roots are brown and hairy, unlike the more familiar white roots, so it can be hard to tell live roots from dead ones. Dead roots are hollow, and you can peel away the outer covering, leaving an inner wiry core. Remove dead roots when you are repotting. Also, carefully cut away any dead rhizome at the back of the plant, which has supported the oldest growths.

A plant can often be returned to the same size pot; remember to position it near the back of the pot so that there is room at the front for the new growths to spread.

Wear gloves when using Rockwool for repotting. Water the plant to wet the old Rockwool before you remove the plant from its old pot.

2

Tease out the old Rockwool from around the roots and cut away any dead ones.

1

REPOTTING A PHRAGMIPEDIUM

YOU WILL NEED:

◆ Compost, either natural (fir bark chips, medium grade) or synthetic (Rockwool). Wet the Rockwool to avoid breathing in the fibers

◆ Craft knife or sharp pruning shears

◆ Polystyrene chips or other drainage material if using fir bark compost

◆ New pot

◆ Protective gloves and mask, if using Rockwool

Many paphiopedilums are slow growing and do not propagate or divide regularly. It is better not to divide the plant unless it has several new growths that were produced in one season. Always leave three or four growths on a plant.

Phragmipediums

Phragmipediums are robust and can get very large, especially when more than one new growth is produced in a year. Do not repot annually, only when they are large enough to be divided. Do this in spring, when they have the summer to grow. Those plants that stay in bloom for many months should have their flowering curtailed to ensure a speedy recovery after repotting.

Phragmipediums have a vigorous root system and should be put into large pots. When repotting, you won't need to trim the live roots unless they are extremely long. For best results use Rockwool; there is no need to use any drainage material.

Set the plant in its new pot, wet the Rockwool, and pack it fairly loosely around the orchid so that the roots can penetrate it easily.

Paphiopedilums and phragmipediums look similar but they have different potting and watering requirements.

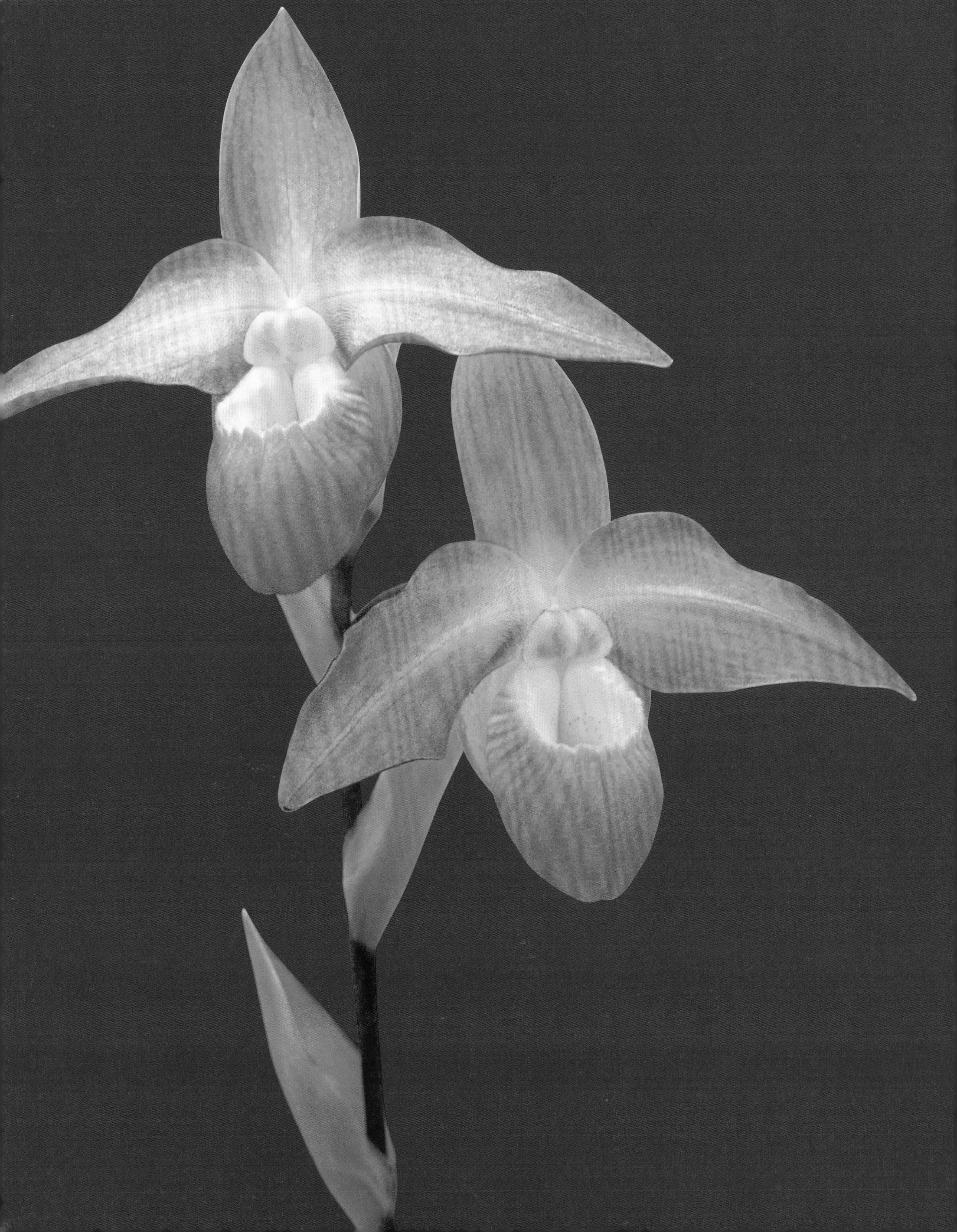

◀ *Phragmipedium* Don Wimber

This strong, robust hybrid produces its orange-red blooms in succession along a tall, ever-growing flower spike. The plant can, therefore, remain in bloom for several months at a time. The rich coloring is a direct result of the influence of one species, *Phragmipedium besseae*.

▼ *Paphiopedilum* Barbarita

Known as a complex type hybrid, this clone produces a single large flower richly colored in gold and copper. The large dorsal sepal, which is yellow and white and peppered with dark brown, dominates the flower. These hybrids will bloom for many weeks during the winter.

Paphiopedilum Maudiae ▶

This lovely flower combines grace and elegance. A
single bloom is produced on a tall flower spike. The
flower is dominated by the spreading dorsal sepal at
the top, which is veined in the same clear green as
the petals and pouch. This lovely plant with mottled
foliage is an old hybrid.

Phragmipedium Sorcerer's Apprentice ▼

This robust and appealing hybrid produces very tall flower
spikes—over 3 feet (1 m) when fully grown. The flowers are
produced over many months, with just one or two open at
any time. The magical blooms are large, exciting,
and contain various shades of red, orange, and gold.

Paphiopedilum Raisin Jack ▶

Raised along similar lines to *Paphiopedilum* Jack Flash (below), this hybrid shows a more open flower, with the petals held almost horizontally, facing away from the pouch. The wide dorsal sepal is flamed with green and purple, which matches the coloring of the petals and pouch.

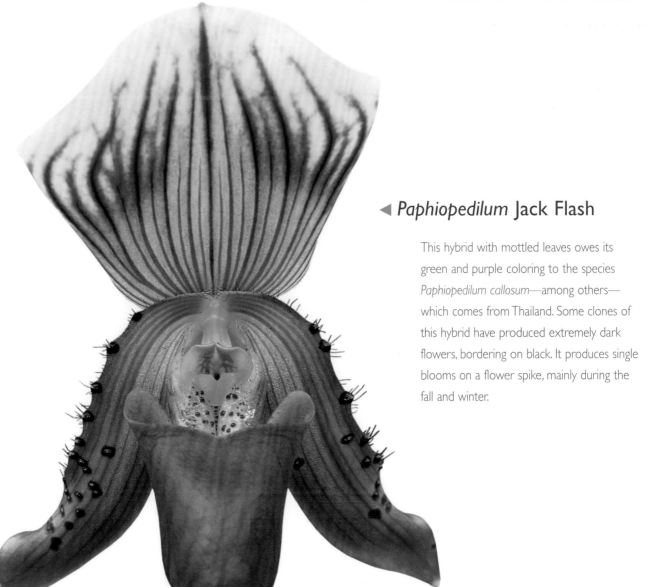

◀ *Paphiopedilum* Jack Flash

This hybrid with mottled leaves owes its green and purple coloring to the species *Paphiopedilum callosum*—among others—which comes from Thailand. Some clones of this hybrid have produced extremely dark flowers, bordering on black. It produces single blooms on a flower spike, mainly during the fall and winter.

▼ *Paphiopedilum insigne*

This species originates in the Himalayas and was at one time cultivated for the cut flower trade. Once extremely common in collections, it became a rare collector's item, but is now more widely available thanks to advances in propagation that have allowed it to be produced for non-specialist nurseries and garden centers.

Paphiopedilum Leeanum ▶

This is an old-style hybrid developed over one hundred years ago. Still popular today, the single bloom combines the qualities of two species, *Paphiopedilum spicerianum* and *Paphiopedilum insigne*. The plant has neat, plain green foliage.

Paphiopedilum Helvetia ▶

By creative hybridizing, using the multi-flowered species, some very fine hybrids have appeared, which produce sprays of flowers on upright flower spikes. In this hybrid, the narrow, sweeping petals give shape and character to these light yellow blooms. They are extremely long lasting and will bloom mainly during the winter.

◀ *Paphiopedilum* Actaeus

Sometimes considered an acquired taste, like good wine, this strong, imposing bloom with its assertive chocolate-brown coloring has great appeal to connoisseurs. Produced singly on a flower spike, the dramatic 4-inch- (10-cm-) wide bloom will last for many weeks during the winter.

◄ *Paphiopedilum* Tear Drop

A comparatively new line of breeding has produced yet another type of attractive flower within this variable genus. Here, a single golden yellow bloom, with a green-yellow dorsal sepal, gives a well balanced outline. As this flower fades, another will take its place on the same flower spike in an ongoing succession.

Paphiopedilum Les Laveurs ▼

This modern classic hybrid produces well-rounded flowers with wide petals and a heavy dorsal sepal surrounding a deep red pouch. The petals are attractively colored in two-tone red-bronze and are highly glossed, as if varnished. The plant has plain green foliage.

miltoniopsis

Affectionately called **Pansy Orchids, Miltoniopsis** have large, flat blooms with a prominent and colorful lip, and most are fragrant. The species are all high-altitude, epiphytic plants that grow mainly on trees. Although a small genus with only a few species, these have had an enormous impact on today's houseplant orchids, since they have produced many rich and colorful hybrids that have proved easy to grow indoors. These hybrids range from white through many shades of pink to deep crimson red and yellow. **Miltoniopsis** are distinguished from all other orchids by their large decorative lip. At the center is a butterfly-shaped mask, or honey guide, whose purpose is to attract pollinating insects. The mask is often surrounded by bold striping or other vivid markings, the loveliest of which is the water droplet (or waterfall) design that splashes over the lip.

Miltoniopsis (Mil-<u>tone</u>-ee-op-sis)

Common name Pansy Orchid. Five species, mostly from Colombia. Genus name established in 1889; only commonly used from 1976. Many varied hybrids cultivated; the species are rare.

all about miltoniopsis

Miltoniopsis, with their sweet pansylike faces, come in many brilliant colors. Keep them indoors and out of direct sun—perhaps alongside a phalaenopsis since they like the same conditions—and they will provide a spectacular display once or twice a year.

Bright and pretty, the blooms of Miltoniopsis last three or four weeks.

Miltoniopsis have light green, oval pseudobulbs with a single apex leaf and two basal leaves that partially sheath the pseudobulb. The narrow oval leaves are light green, sometimes turning to blue-green. Flower spikes are produced from the base of the leading pseudobulb and start within the protection of the basal leaf. Once they emerge from the leaf, they can be supported and trained upright. The flower spikes, often two to a pseudobulb, do grow not much taller than the foliage and can carry up to six 4-inch- (10-cm-) wide flowers. The petals and sepals are equal in size and the gaily patterned lip is double their size.

Miltoniopsis have one main flowering season, usually in early summer, but in fall they will often come into flower again and the blooms will last for three to four weeks. They regularly produce more than one new growth in a season, quite quickly becoming large, multi-leaded plants that will give several flower spikes at the same time, or in succession, as the new growths mature into pseudobulbs.

Starting small

These accommodating plants are often available from specialist nurseries as young seedlings, or mericlones. If you have the patience to wait two or three years, it can be fun to bring a plant to maturity and to see the new pseudobulbs get larger with each passing season. If you purchase seedlings, you won't be sure of the exact coloring of the flowers or their markings until they bloom.

Miltoniopsis can flower while only two to three years old, but it is best to remove the flower spike and encourage the plant to put on new growth instead. If you can't resist seeing the bloom, allow the plant to produce one flower, then cut it off as soon as it opens and new growth will follow. The flowers produced by young plants will not be their best but will give some idea of the joy to come.

CARING FOR MILTONIOPSIS

Miltoniopsis do best indoors when grown alongside phalaenopsis in a minimum temperature of 55°F (13°C). They do not have a definite resting period and can receive the same treatment all year.

These shade-loving plants should never be put in direct sun. Too much light is bad for their soft foliage and may cause spotting or yellowing of the leaves. For the same reason it is better not to spray the foliage regularly. Instead, give an occasional wipe with a damp tissue to keep the foliage clean. Never withhold water for so long that the plants dry out and the pseudobulbs begin to shrivel. Although the plants should not be allowed to become completely dry, they must not be overwatered either. Too much water will cause the soft new growths to rot, and the rot can run through the whole plant.

Repot as you would cymbidiums (see pp. 44–5). Miltoniopsis have a fine rooting system and prefer to be kept in as small a pot as possible. They do well with regular repotting, about once every two years, and often need only to be dropped into the next size pot without disturbing the root ball.

HELPFUL HINTS

SITE
Warm room indoors, with a minimum temperature of 55°F (13°C), away from direct sun.

OUTDOORS OR IN?
Never put outdoors, even in summer.

CARE
Keep watered all year round, but do not overwater. Wipe the leaves rather than spray the plant.

WHEN TO REPOT
Repot after flowering, every two years.

SIZE
Adult plants no more than about 18 inches (45 cm) high. Blooms are up to 4 inches (10 cm) across.

Miltoniopsis Venus

Pale pink flowers with yellow centers combine with a pattern of crimson stripes and dots, radiating down through the lip. This was the first of the waterfall miltoniopsis—raised nearly 100 years ago. The parents are *M. vexillaria,* which gives the pink color, and *M. phalaenopsis,* which contributes the waterfall effect.

Miltoniopsis Rozel

Petals and sepals of deep burgundy are enhanced by a
white lip with burgundy borders displaying a pronounced
waterfall pattern. This hybrid originates from the Eric
Young Orchid Foundation in Jersey in the Channel Islands,
a nursery of repute recognized worldwide, and is named
after a scenic local area. These orchids make excellent
houseplants and, if well cared for, can flower twice a year.

◄ *Miltoniopsis* Plemont Point

The mainly white flowers have a splash of light crimson on the petals. The marking on the lip is the same color as the petals and is known as the mask. The golden center, or honey guide, is nature's way of directing insects to the center of the flower.

Miltoniopsis Jersey ▼

Petals and lip are both plum-red, with the points of the sepals picked out in white. The whole flower looks like velvet, soft and deep. The attractive foliage is a delicate gray-green, indicating that the plant, whose original species grows in the Colombian rain forests, must always be kept out of direct sun.

SITE
Warm room indoors, away from direct sun.

OUTDOORS OR IN?
Do not put outdoors, even in summer.

CARE
Keep watered all year round, but do not overwater.

WHEN TO REPOT
Repot after flowering, once every two years.

SIZE
Adult plants are never more than about 18 inches (45 cm) high. Blooms are up to 4 inches (10 cm) wide.

▲ *Miltoniopsis* Nancy Binks

In this orchid, the rose-pink petals curl back slightly, with the center vein picked out in dark port wine. Here the waterfall effect has merged to give solid color and the lip has a convex shape.

◀ *Miltoniopsis* Hudson Bay

This white flower with bold splashes of color has a lip delicately marked with dark pink. Even a modest-sized plant will produce a succession of flowers. Here, two more spikes with young buds are waiting to open. These blooms will remain in perfect condition for six to eight weeks.

Miltoniopsis vexillaria ▶

Now extremely rare, this fragrant, salmon pink species is a collector's item. It is a treasure to be found in the background of most of today's hybrids.

◀ *Miltoniopsis* Herralexandre

Large, creamy yellow flowers with distinctive yellow and purple patterning mark this hybrid.

miltonias and brassias

Miltonias have recently become popular largely because of their ability to hybridize, especially with brassias. Neither is a large genus, and the hybrids available today are the result of close breeding with only a few species to create a wonderful new range of exciting plants in the *Odontoglossum* Alliance. Brassias are the more robust of the two. Miltonias are smaller than many orchids, and the species often have just one or two blooms out at a time, in a long-lasting succession. Hybridizing with brassias has increased their size and the number of blooms. These new hybrids are very vigorous and can tolerate a wide range of temperatures. Among their notable qualities are stunning blooms on tall flower spikes, which in *Brassia* hybrids display subtle pastel shades as well as green and brown, while those with strong *Miltonia* influence revel in bright hues bordering on red and brown.

Miltonia (Mil-<u>tone</u>-ee-ah)

Common name Pansy Orchid. Named for Viscount Milton, a Yorkshireman and early 19th-century orchid grower. Genus established in 1837. Ten species, mostly from Brazil (see photo, p. 95).

Brassia (<u>Bras</u>-ee-ah)

Common name: Spider Orchid. Named for botanical artist William Brass. Genus established in 1813. Thirty-five species from tropical Central and South America (see photo, left).

all about miltonia and brassia hybrids

The variety and vigor of these orchids have been greatly enhanced by hybridization to produce gorgeous orchids that thrive in the home.

High in the Costa Rican rain forest, this *Brassia* has the characteristic spidery petals of the species.

A shady position indoors with an intermediate temperature range suits these hybrids best. The good-looking plants are robust, with oval to oblong shiny green pseudobulbs, topped with a pair of long, narrow apex leaves. They rapidly grow into large specimens that need a big pot—up to 10 inches (25 cm) in size—to contain them. You can control their size by dividing the plants every three or four years, but if you have enough space, a larger plant will give a better display, with several flower spikes in full bloom at any one time.

Flowering

Brassias are known as Spider Orchids because of the spiderlike appearance of the flowers. The narrow sepals and petals of these amazing, fragrant blooms can measure 4–5 inches (10–12 cm) long. The pure *Brassia* hybrids are dominated by a tantalizing green, often overlaid with a darker color or brown spotting. Pure *Miltonia* hybrids tend to be white or various shades of pink and red, with a decorated lip.

Selective intergeneric breeding of miltonias and brassias over many generations has resulted in hybrids with an amazing variety of shapes and colors. Because of their complicated makeup, the plants tend to bloom at various times of the year, except for the true brassias, which bloom during the summer. All these orchids remain in flower for at least four to six weeks.

Repotting

Repot these plants every two years as you would cymbidiums (see pp. 44–45). If they are left in the same pot for too long, their large pseudobulbs will jut over the edge of the pot and their roots will grow outside it. This makes the plants harder to manage and subjects them to unnecessary stress.

Divide the hybrids when they get too large and heavy for you to pick up easily. Leave at least three pseudobulbs and one new growth on each division. Cut off the older backbulbs when you repot the orchid and pot them separately. In this way you can use them to create more plants, which should bloom within four to five years.

THE STORY OF A HYBRID

Possibly the most stunning of the intergeneric hybrids is *Beallara* (see p. 103), a quadrigeneric genus. Behind this successful man-made genus are *Miltonia* x *Brassia* x *Odontoglossum* x *Cochlioda*. Plants with this breeding produce tall flower spikes with up to a dozen 3¹/₂-inch (9-cm), star-shaped flowers. The sepals are pointed and the petals centrally patterned in the attractive manner of almost all odontoglossums. The lip is large and flared, and variously decorated. Red splashes on a white background is a frequently seen and much admired combination.

BRASSIAS
(main photo)
HELPFUL HINTS

SITE
Windowsill indoors
with good light, but
away from direct sun.
At night, a minimum
temperature of 55°F
(13°C); maximum
daytime temperature
of 86°F (30°C).

OUTDOORS OR IN?
Never put outdoors.

CARE
Keep lightly watered
and feed all year
round, but less often
in winter.

WHEN TO REPOT
Repot every two
years, after flowering.
Divide if necessary.

SIZE
Adult plants up to
about 18 inches
(45 cm) tall. Petals
and sepals up to
6 inches (15 cm) long.

MILTONIAS
HELPFUL HINTS

SITE
Windowsill indoors
with good light, but
away from direct sun.
Minimum nighttime
temperature of 55°F
(13°C); maximum
daytime temperature
of 86°F (30°C).

OUTDOORS OR IN?
Never put outdoors,
even in summer.

CARE
Keep lightly watered
and feed all year
round, but less often
in winter.

WHEN TO REPOT
Repot every two
years, after flowering.
Divide if necessary.

SIZE
Adult plants up to
about 18 inches
(45 cm) tall. Flowers
up to 4 inches
(10 cm) across.

Beallara Tahoma Glacier ▶

A complex hybrid, containing four genera: *Brassia*,
Cochlioda, *Miltonia*, and *Odontoglossum*. The *Brassia*
influence can be seen in the arching habit and pointed
petals and sepals; the *Miltonia* has contributed the bold
central coloring of this striking creation.

Sanderara Rippon Tor ▲

This is a tri-generic hybrid, produced by crossings of
Brassia, *Cochlioda*, and *Odontoglossum*. Little remains of the
Brassia influence, except perhaps the arching habit.
Otherwise, this complex hybrid looks more like its
Odontoglossum forebear.

HELPFUL HINTS

SITE
Windowsill indoors
with good light, but
away from direct sun.
At night, minimum
temperature of 55°F
(13°C); maximum
daytime temperature
of 86°F (30°C).

OUTDOORS OR IN?
Never put outdoors,
even in summer.

CARE
Keep lightly watered
and feed all year
round, but less often
in winter.

WHEN TO REPOT
Repot every two
years, after flowering.

SIZE
Adult plants (true
brassias) up to about
18 inches (45 cm)
tall. Petals and sepals
up to 6 inches
(15 cm) long.

▲ *Brassia* Rex

This is a much earlier hybrid, but it remains very popular.
It is typical of the genus. The flowers show extremely
narrow sepals and petals that are light green, with darker
spotting toward the center of the blooms. These flower
spikes must be left to arch naturally and gracefully for the
flowers to be seen at their best.

◀ *McLellanara* St. Ouen

Brassia, *Oncidium*, and *Odontoglossum*
combine to make this decorative clone an
instant success. The base color is creamy
yellow, with chocolate brown patterning
on the sepals and petals. It is a tall-
flowered and robustly growing plant.

◄ *Miltonia spectabile*

This handsome flower is a species from Brazil that, although rare today, has become a highly successful parent of exquisite hybrids. When crossed with *Brassia*, the resulting genus is known as *Miltassia*.

Brassia Edvah Loo ►

The extraordinary blooms of this Spider Orchid have extended petals that reach 6 inches (15 cm) below the lip. The flowers have elegantly elongated, light yellow-green petals and sepals, with a pointed white lip. Beautifully regimented along the spike, the flowers create a marvelous asymmetric design.

the cattleya alliance

Cattleyas are seldom simply cattleyas! They are foremost in a huge group of interrelated plants known as the *Cattleya* Alliance. This group includes numerous natural genera such as *Laelia* and *Sophronitis*, as well as many man-made genera. All of these come under the general umbrella of cattleyas, and all require the same conditions and care. Cattleyas are mostly epiphytic plants originating in Central and South America. In their natural environment, they can grow into huge specimens more than 3 feet (1 m) across, and such amazing sights were common in tropical forests during the early days of orchid exploration. Among the species, the main colorings are pink, lavender, and cerise, as well as white and yellow. Hybridization has intensified and broadened this color range. The flowers are undeniably gorgeous, large and flashy with exceptionally showy lips, all frills and fancy markings, and a sparkling, crystalline quality. The flowers were so often portrayed on boxes of candy that they became fondly known as Chocolate Box Orchids.

Cattleya (Kat-lee-ya)

Common name Chocolate Box Orchid. Once described as the King of Orchids. Named for William Cattley, an early horticulturalist. Genus established in 1821. About 50 species from South America. Today, intergeneric hybrids mostly grown.

all about cattleyas

The magnificent, long-lasting flowers and the ease with which the orchids can be grown account for the popularity of cattleyas. Taller types, with two leaves, have more, smaller flowers than those with a single leaf, which bear much larger flowers.

Robust plants, cattleyas produce stout, elongated pseudobulbs with one or two thick, leathery, oval leaves, depending on the type. They range in size from the miniature varieties that are no more than 6 inches (15 cm) high to the tallest at 2 feet (60 cm), and all sizes in between.

Short flower spikes, carrying up to four fragrant blooms, emerge from the apex of the pseudobulb at the base of the leaf. They are protected in their early stage of development by a green sheath that splits along its length as the buds swell to fill it before bursting out. The flowers can remain in perfect condition for up to four weeks. They are 2–5 inches (10–13 cm) across, with petals and sepals about the same size, and a large lip usually dominates the flower. Typically, the lip flares out with an exotic frilled edge, beautifully stained with contrasting colors, most commonly purple.

Cattleyas have a thickened rhizome that is clearly visible at the base of the plant. The pseudobulbs are spread out along this with about 1 inch (2.5 cm) between them. The plants develop a thick, strong rooting system, which often does not start growing until the newest pseudobulb is partially mature. Cattleyas tend to spread out as they grow and their roots often hang over the rim of the pot. Once this happens, any new roots will be aerial and hang down like a thick, white beard. Cattleyas can grow

in this fashion for several years until they are finally repotted, when you can divide them to control their size. The larger the plant, the better the flower display, but very large plants are more difficult to handle because they become very heavy.

Cattleyas are seasonal in their growing and flowering habit, with most types blooming at the same time each year, usually in either spring or fall. Not many cattleyas bloom during the warmer summer months, when their pseudobulbs are still developing. Many start their new growth in fall rather than in spring, and bloom about twelve months later.

Today, there is great choice among cattleyas, with many new varieties to amaze and excite. Look for the smaller, trim hybrids, which take up less room.

Bright cherry red blooms make *Laeliocattleya* Secret Love justifiably popular. This semi-miniature, bifoliate hybrid blooms in summer and the flowers will last for as long as three weeks.

GROWING WILD

Cattleya violacea, a once plentiful species, is rare today. The plants are found in tropical forests in South and Central America, where they grow on tree branches, their thick roots firmly gripping the bark. High in the canopy, they are protected from bright sun by the leaves above them. In the dry season they rest, getting more light as the trees shed some of their foliage.

HELPFUL HINTS

SITE
Warm room indoors
with a minimum
temperature of 55°F
(13°C) at night. Bright
light away from direct
sunlight.

OUTDOORS OR IN?
Outdoors in summer
in tropical climates.

CARE
Water sparingly
when resting; water
generously when
growing. Spray leaves
in summer.

WHEN TO REPOT
After flowering, when
the plant has
outgrown its pot.

SIZE
Adult plants range
from 6 inches
(15 cm) to 2 feet
(60 cm) high. Blooms
are 2–5 inches
(10–13 cm) across.

caring for cattleyas

These are seasonal orchids, with definite growing and resting periods, but each plant has its own cycle, which dictates how you should care for it.

Cattleya showing new growth just starting at the base (to the right of the stem), with a dormant secondary eye (to the left of the stem), which will grow only if the new growth becomes damaged.

Cattleyas are intermediate orchids that like good light, doing best where temperatures sometimes reach a low of 55°F (13°C) for part of the year. In summer they thrive in temperatures of up to 86°F (30°C). High temperatures demand high humidity, which can be difficult to maintain in the home; a sunroom is an ideal place for cattleyas.

Although the orchids need good light in order to bloom well, *Cattleya* leaves are liable to scorching if they are exposed to direct sun. In tropical climates, you can grow them outdoors for much of the time, beneath an awning. Spray them regularly to provide humidity.

In cooler parts of the world, cattleyas are not as easy to grow, but by providing the right amount of light, humidity, and temperature, cattleyas can thrive in the home.

Watering around the year

After flowering, the plant will go into its resting period, which may last for weeks or even months. Aerial roots outside the pot will cease to grow and their green, growing tips will become sheathed with velamen, a white papery covering. During this time, give only enough water to keep the pseudobulbs plump. As a guide, reduce the watering to about half; this means that for most of the time the plant will be a little dry. If the pseudobulbs begin to shrivel, the plant is too dry.

After its rest, triggered by light or higher temperatures, the plant will produce a fat new growth from the base of the previous pseudobulb. At about the same time, the roots will regrow. This is the signal to start watering normally again. It is also the right time to repot the plant if necessary—repot as you would a *Cymbidium* (see pp. 44–5). Apply feed at every second watering.

After repotting, give limited water until the new roots start to grow, and from then on be generous; cattleyas need plenty of water while they are growing. You can mist or spray the foliage when the temperature is warm enough, but be sure not to get water into the new growth or down between the leaf and its sheath.

Toward the end of the growing season, the new pseudobulbs that have been developing over the

WATERING CATTLEYAS

Stage of growth	Amount of water	Feed
Resting	Just enough to keep pseudobulbs plump	No
New leaves and roots beginning to grow	Give plenty of water; mist or spray foliage in warm temperatures	Every second watering
Flowers open	Keep plant fairly dry	Every second watering
After repotting	Give little water until new roots start to grow	Every second watering

Without removing the plant from its pot, sever the rhizome as shown to make two plants from one. Leave at least four pseudobulbs on each half. Do this in the fall and by spring new growth will have started on both divisions. Then plant them in separate pots.

previous months should be plump and as big as the previous ones. If a pseudobulb appears smaller, it is a sign that the plant is not happy in its surroundings, and you may need to find another place where it will grow better. If a large pseudobulb is growing at an angle, it may need some support from a cane to keep it upright.

While buds are developing, keep the foliage dry to prevent the buds from turning yellow at an early stage. Once the flowers have opened, keep the plant on the dry side and out of bright light. This will encourage the blooms to last longer. If the humidity is high while the plant is in bloom, the flowers will quickly become spotted and disfigured by the dampness.

Dividing cattleyas

Cattleyas are robust growers and will often produce several new growths that will branch out in different directions to make a multi-leaded plant. At this stage, you may want to divide it into smaller, individual plants, but make sure that any division retains at least four pseudobulbs. If you think ahead and sever the woody rhizome between the

pseudobulbs (see above) six months before you actually repot it, you will put less strain on the plant. By the time you repot it, the plant will be thriving again. Any backbulbs that you have severed from the main plant will already have started to make new growth—giving the bonus of a newly propagated division to grow separately.

▼ *Laeliocattleya* Drumbeat

This is the typical coloring for these flamboyant orchids. The frilled petals match the soft lavender of the sepals, while the frilled lip is deep crimson with two small yellow highlights toward the center. This is a unifoliate variety, which means that it produces a single leaf on each of its pseudobulbs.

Brassolaeliocattleya Fortumate ▶

This exquisite, single colored bloom illustrates how an unadorned flower can be as striking as any color combination. Here, the flowers are a rich, glowing yellow, which is a shade hard to find in this genus. The lip is small and rounded, producing a well-balanced flower.

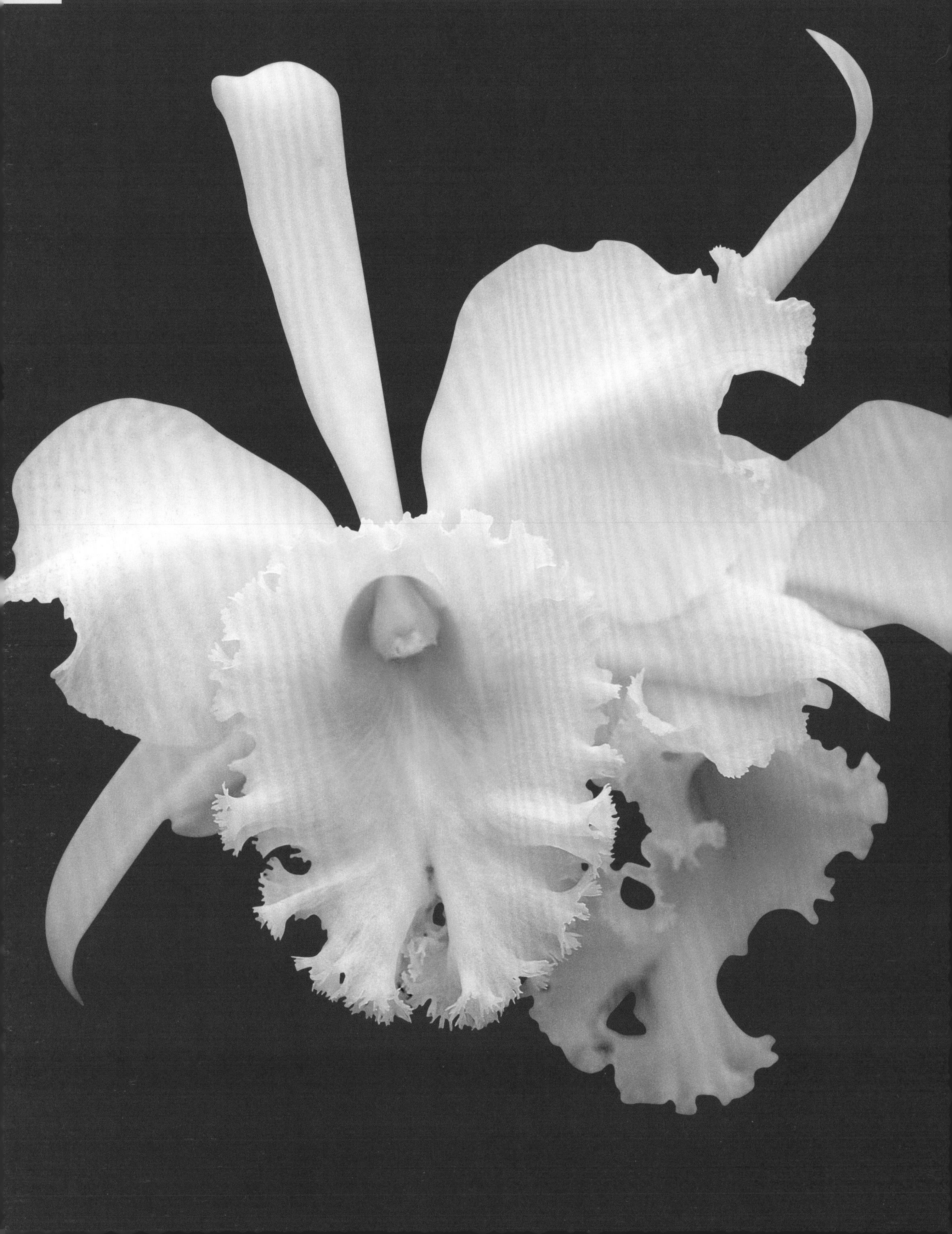

◄ *Brassolaeliocattleya* Albion

The frilled lip and wavy outline of this virgin white flower
betray the plant's origins within *Brassavola digbyana*, a
species once used to provide large, flamboyant hybrids
such as this. Although this orchid is far removed from the
original species, the characteristics are still evident.

▼ *Cattleya* Amethyst Rose

These elegant, slender-petaled blooms reveal a likeness to
the original species from which this hybrid is not very far
removed. The modestly sized blooms are white with a
slight pink blush, while the lip is brushed with salmon
pink. This is a bifoliate type, bearing two leaves on each of
its pseudobulbs.

Cattleya Winter's Lace

A large-flowered variety, this orchid can
produce up to four blooms on a flower spike.
The soft, cloud-white bloom is embellished
with a touch of gold at the center of the lip.

Potinara Rebecca Merkel

The results can be stunning when another dimension is added to the trio of *Cattleya*, *Laelia*, and *Brassovola*. The addition of the red species *Sophronitis coccinia* has produced this remarkably rich red hybrid. The flowers are smaller than those of many in this alliance, but the rich coloring ensures that this lovely clone is a winner.

◄ *Laeliocattleya* Breen's Jenny Ann

Known as a semi-alba, this wonderful red and white bloom results from using albino forms of the species to produce a line of white or semi-alba clones. The petals are milk white, without any trace of color, while the lip is almost completely crimson. The only other decoration is a yellow stain in the center of the bloom.

Laeliocattleya Elizabeth Fulton ►

This charming orchid exhibits a remarkable contrast in colors, with the solid crimson lip standing out against the green-gold sepals and burnt honey yellow petals. The small, compact lip lacks the frills of many cattleyas.

◄ *Cattleya* Bahaiana

A highly decorative hybrid, this orchid produces four flowers on a spike. The blooms are not very large for the genus, but the sepals are gaily patterned with red spotting over a light-colored base. The unusual petals mimic the lip, so the bloom looks as though it has three lips.

Laeliocattleya Ocarina 'Fascination' ▼

The exquisite yellow coloring of this delightful bloom, with wide, generous petals, sets off the deep crimson lip, which has a copper-gold overlay on the edge. The large flowers last up to four weeks in perfect condition if kept cool and well shaded.

Brassolaeliocattleya Memoria Dorothy Bertsch ▼

Of similar breeding to *Brassolaeliocattleya Albion*, this clean-lined hybrid lacks its frills. Instead, it has narrow petals and sepals with a delicately colored, rounded lip. These orchids can become fairly large with stout pseudobulbs, and need considerable space in which to grow.

Laeliocattleya Pandora Bracey ▶

This lovely clone is known as a splash-petal type because a dash of the rich mauve coloring of the lip is repeated across the showy petals. To enjoy these delightful blooms at their best, support the flower spike with a cane. The flowers will last for about three weeks.

dendrobiums

Dendrobiums belong to one of the largest genera in the orchid family. With such a huge number of species, their appearance and growing habits vary greatly. This chapter covers two main groups of hybrids that are produced for the mass market. The first group, the soft-caned dendrobiums, have been bred from a small number of Indian species, the most important of which is *Dendrobium nobile*. Their long, leafy pseudobulbs are called canes. Their colorful and perfectly rounded flowers come in shades of white, pink, yellow, and mauve. The second group, the hard-caned dendrobiums, illustrated on this page, have tough, rigid canes and are hybrids of various species from Australia and New Guinea. Their flowers are in a wider range of shapes in white, yellow, pink verging on dark mauve, and an extraordinary rich, royal purple.

Dendrobium (Den-dro-bee-um)

Common name: Bamboo Orchid. From the Greek, meaning "living on a tree." Genus established in 1799. Nine hundred species are known from China to New Zealand. Some species and many hybrids are grown.

all about dendrobiums

In the wild, the species from which modern hybrids are descended cling to tree branches, with their canes trailing below. The hybrids will do the same, displaying their epiphytic origins, unless they are tied upright as they grow.

Dendrobiums are among the loveliest of orchid plants, with shiny green leaves and fresh-looking canes.

Soft-caned dendrobiums

Soft-caned *Dendrobium* hybrids produce long, cane-like, segmented pseudobulbs up to 18 inches (45 cm) tall, which are sheathed in short, oval leaves. The canes and leaves are mid-green, with the oldest canes turning yellow and shriveling with age. Most modern hybrids lose the leaves from the older pseudobulbs after two to three years.

One or two flowers appear in spring and early summer on short stems, which can arise along the entire length of the latest matured pseudobulb on the side opposite the leaf. Older canes can continue to flower until all the eyes, or embryo buds, have developed. The blooms have sepals and petals of equal size, and have a round lip. Typical coloring is white, with a pink or mauve overlay at the petal tips; the lip often has a boldly colored central disc and a yellow highlight. The roots are thin, white, and numerous and may grow over the rim of the pot.

Hard-caned dendrobiums

The second group of dendrobiums also have tall pseudobulbs known as canes. They are less fleshy and their leaves cover two-thirds of their length. The mid- to dark-green, stiff pointed leaves are oval. The plants are 12 inches (30 cm) to 2 feet (60 cm) tall.

In spring and early summer, flower spikes grow at the top of the matured cane; these can be up to 12 inches (30 cm) long and carry a spray of a dozen 2-inch- (5-cm-) wide, richly colored flowers that last for several weeks. Sometimes the sepals and petals are the same size as the small, pointed lip. On other plants, sepals and petals are narrow and twisting and yellow is often seen with a contrasting red to mauve lip.

Hard-caned dendrobiums retain their foliage for several years before discarding several leaves at once. A healthy plant should have most of its canes in leaf at any one time.

The stunning yellow flower spike of *Dendrobium* Thongchia Gold shows to advantage when staked upright.

WILD ANCESTORS

In the wild, dendrobiums come in many shapes and sizes—from diminutive species like this New Guinea example a few inches (cm) high to tall Asian giants, which can reach 4–5 feet (120–150 cm). All grow as epiphytes upon trees, often surviving long droughts with moisture stored up in their canes. Many become leafless during dry periods.

Dendrobium vannouhuusii

HELPFUL HINTS

SITE
Windowsill with bright light, no direct sun. Sunroom or heated greenhouse in winter.
Hard caned: minimum temperature of 64°F (18°C); soft caned: 50°F (10°C). Summer maximum of 86°F (30°) for both.

OUTDOORS OR IN?
Never put outdoors, even in summer.

CARE
Spray and water all summer but do not overwater. Do not water in winter.

WHEN TO REPOT
Repot after flowering, every two years.

SIZE
Adult plants are never more than 18 inches (45 cm) high. Blooms are up to 4 inches (10 cm) across.

caring for dendrobiums

The key to success with these seasonal orchids is to provide plenty of light and a marked contrast in light and temperature between the summer growing season and the winter resting period.

In tropical climates, the hard-caned types do best due to the higher temperatures and year-round light. This agrees with their need for a fast growing season, followed by a long rest period.

In temperate regions, they need a warm spot with a nighttime minimum of 64°F (18°C). For cooler-growing soft-caned hybrids, the winter temperature can drop to 50°F (10°C) at night and rise by day to at least 59°F (15°C). In summer, they need daytime temperatures up to 86°F (30°C) so that their long canes can mature during the growing season and bloom again the next spring.

PROPAGATING A DENDROBIUM

Propagation is seldom achieved with the hard-caned dendrobiums, but it can be exciting to produce new plants from the soft-caned hybrids. Choose an unflowered, but leafless, older cane, which is still green and plump. Cut it down to the base and divide it into 2-inch (5-cm) lengths with a sharp knife. Dip each severed end in powdered sulfur to dry up the area and prevent rotting. Fill a pot halfway with compost and place the cut pieces upright around the edge, pushing them down until the segmented section is level with the compost. Place the pot in a plastic bottle cut in half, and replace the top part (leave off the cap) over the bottom to keep the compost moist. Within a few weeks some of the divisions will start to grow. Your new plants will be flowering in a few years.

Dendrobiums in bloom

Preparation for the spring flowering starts as soon as the canes have matured at the end of summer. Move the orchids to winter quarters with plenty of natural light. The most suitable place may be a sunroom or heated greenhouse, where light from more than one direction can help ripen the canes. The switch from shady summer quarters to a full-light winter home may cause slight yellowing of the foliage. In the spring, when normal watering and feeding starts, the plants will become green again.

Keep the plants on the dry side, watering occasionally only if the pseudobulbs begin to shrivel. Ideally, they should remain plump throughout the winter with very little water. If they do shrivel, the canes will have to plump up in the spring, which will delay the start of their new growths and could affect the flowering.

Spring Care

As spring advances, the buds along the sides of the canes of soft-caned hybrids begin to swell and develop from small green knobs on the segmented pseudobulbs. The flower spikes on hard-caned hybrids start from the top of the matured canes, and continue to grow.

At this stage, give a little water, but don't overdo it. Too much water too soon can cause the embryo buds to convert into adventitious growths, or keikis. As soon as the buds can be easily identified, resume normal watering. When you can see new growths at the base of the plant, you can start to feed it at every other watering. This will encourage any pale foliage to return to a good green color.

As soon as the buds are well advanced, you can move the plant to a room where you can enjoy it. It can remain there until flowering has finished. By now, the new growths should be several inches high, and the plant can be settled in a warm, lightly shaded summer position. Dendrobiums need more light than most orchids while they are growing, but never direct sun. Provided the temperatures are kept up, you can continue to water and apply feed to make sure that the plants continue to grow at a steady rate. You can also spray or mist the foliage regularly to help maintain extra humidity and to balance the temperature, which should now be 10°F (5°C) warmer at night and up to 86°F (30°C) by day.

The canes should have finished growing by the time winter approaches. Continue watering, gradually giving less water, until you see the terminal leaf that indicates that growth is complete.

When to repot

Dendrobiums always appear to be growing in too small a pot, but it is a mistake to repot them in a much larger one, since this can cause overwatering. Repot dendrobiums only when absolutely necessary, immediately after flowering.

The plant on the right is still growing from the apex. The plant on the far right has finished growing, as you can see by the vertical leaf at the apex. This vertical leaf is called a terminal leaf.

A plant may remain in its pot for three or four years without disturbance and still have room for more canes to grow and develop. Be careful not to bury the base of the plant. If the new growths start below the compost, they will probably rot off before reaching the surface. Tie the plants to bamboo canes for support. To prevent the plant from toppling over, place some heavy stones at the bottom of the pot, or set it inside a larger one.

Pot the keiki in a small pot. Later, if necessary, stake it with a bamboo cane to prevent it from falling over.

POTTING A KEIKI

The older eyes may become new plants, known as keikis, instead of flowers. Leave these little plants on the cane until they have roots. Then you can remove them and pot them on their own.

YOU WILL NEED:

◆ dendrobium with keiki
◆ sharp pruning shears or knife
◆ fine bark compost
◆ small pot

1

A keiki is ready to repot when the roots are well developed.

2

Remove the keiki and its roots with sharp pruning shears or a knife.

3

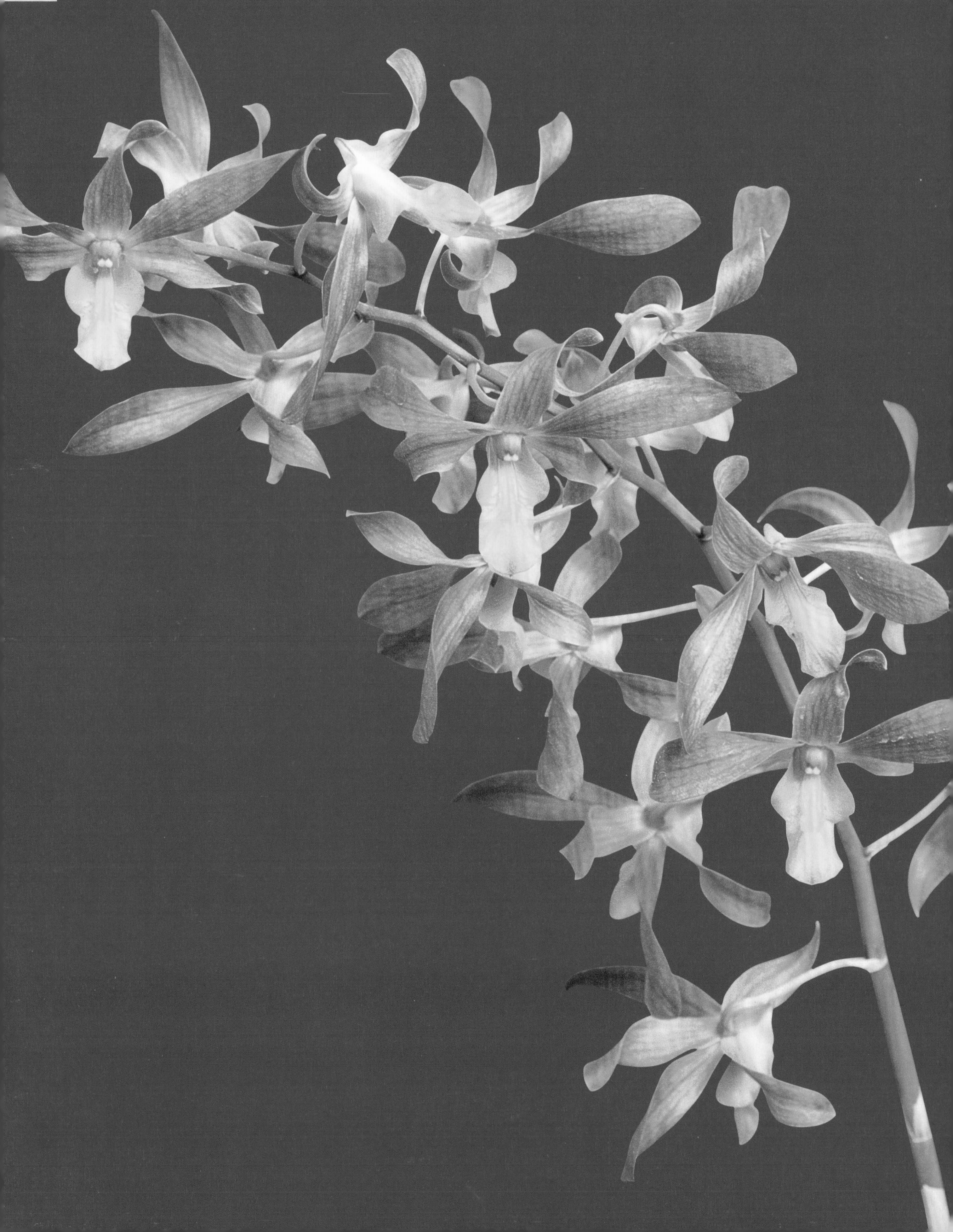

▲ *Dendrobium parishii*

This is a charming, highly perfumed species that originates in Southeast Asia. The plant is small, with canes no longer than 4 inches (10 cm), which often become pendent. It is deciduous, blooming from leafless canes, with one or two rich pink flowers growing from the nodes along the cane.

◄ *Dendrobium* Browne

An attractive variation among the hard-caned dendrobiums, this handsome evergreen hybrid carries tall, upright spikes with many blooms. These have narrow, club-shaped, orange-tan sepals and petals, with a contrasting yellow lip. The petals are twisted, held back to give a flyaway appearance. The plant can grow to 2 feet (60 cm) tall.

HELPFUL HINTS

SITE
Warm room indoors, away from direct sun.

OUTDOORS OR IN
Outside in summer.

CARE
Keep watered in the summer; keep dry in the winter.

WHEN TO REPOT
Repot after flowering.

SIZE
Adult plants are up to 2 feet (60 cm) tall. Blooms are 2 inches (5 cm) or more across.

Dendrobium thyrsiflorum ▶

An evergreen species from India, this orchid produces dainty blooms in long trusses from the top of mature canes. The blooms are white, with a slight hint of pink on the petals and sepals, while the round lip is deep golden yellow. It is a spring-flowering species that grows well on a cool windowsill.

◀ *Dendrobium* Emma White

A lovely variety among the hard-caned dendrobiums, this orchid produces its flowers in sprays from the top portion of the canes. This all-white clone is much admired and praised for the purity of its blooms, which appear in spring and early summer.

Dendrobium senile ▶

This is a miniature type with canes no more than
3 inches (8 cm) tall. The canary yellow blooms appear in
spring and last for three weeks. They are large for the size
of the plant and come from the nodes along the cane.

▼ *Dendrobium* hybrids

These are known as the soft-caned
dendrobiums, and all have been raised
from the species *D. nobile*. This breeding
has produced an abundance of colorful
hybrids ranging from white through cream
to pink and darker red shades. They
bloom in spring and in winter lose some,
but not all, of their foliage.

Dendrobium pierardii ▶

An extremely handsome plant, this orchid produces long, thin canes that quickly droop to 12 inches (30 cm) or more. The plant has a resting period during winter after all foliage has been shed. In spring, the newest canes produce blooms along their entire length. The narrow petals and sepals are soft pink and the rounded lip is creamy white.

▼ *Dendrobium* Trakool Red

This hybrid is among the smallest of the hard-caned dendrobiums. The pseudobulbs are small and slender, about 12 inches (30 cm) tall. The flowers, which are held on spikes well above the foliage, are deep red, with wide petals and a smaller, narrow lip. These lovely blooms will last for several weeks.

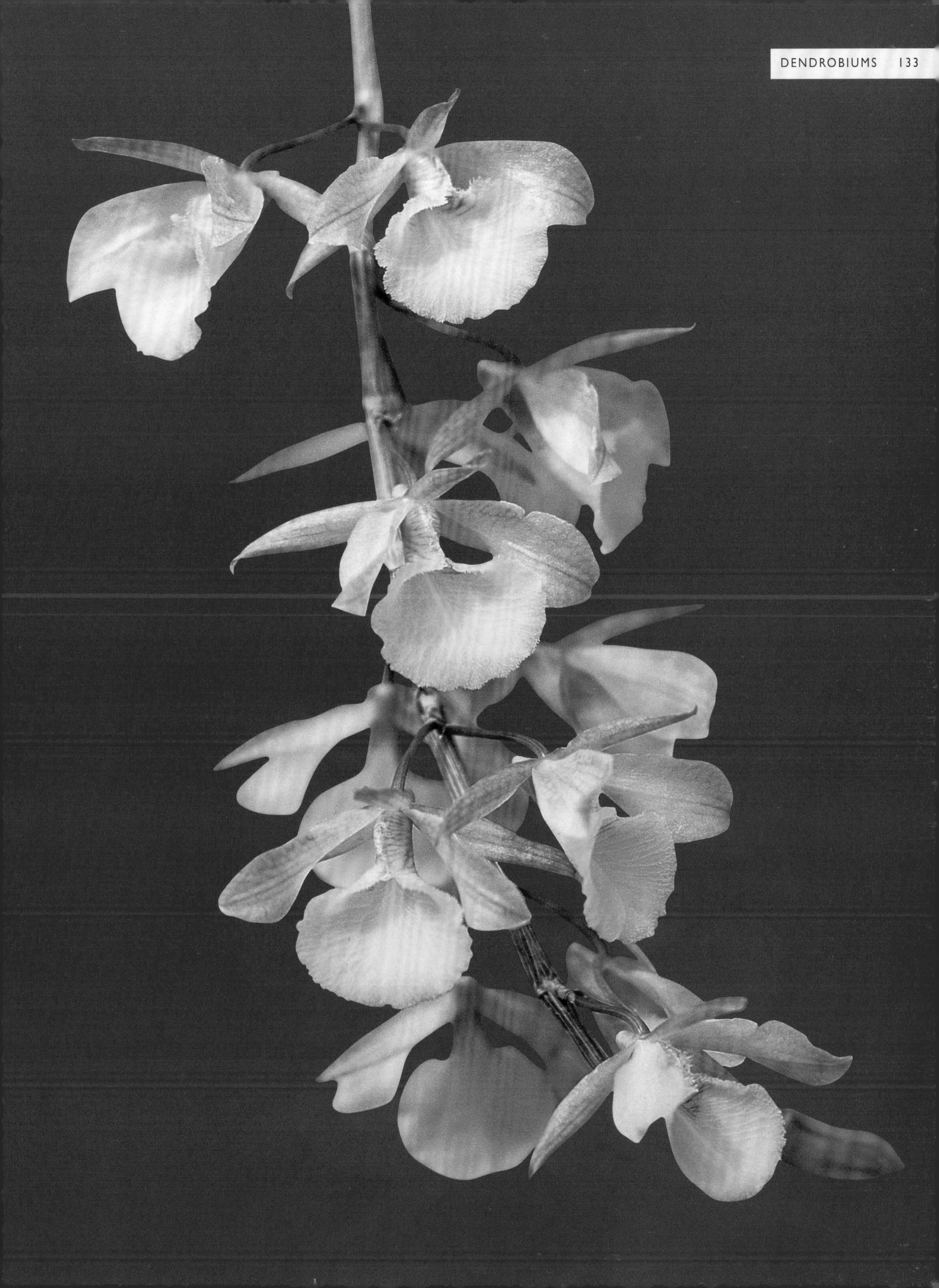

zygopetalums

The main attraction of zygopetalums is the rich coloring of their flowers, which have green, brown-spotted petals and sepals set off by a large, flared lip. The lip itself is white and can be either lightly or densely stained or veined with violet-indigo. This basic coloring makes the plants instantly recognizable when in bloom, although there are some interesting new color variations, such as the green-petaled hybrids. Most zygopetalums are sweetly scented and will last for up to three weeks in bloom. The main flowering season is spring through early summer. The plants produce many leafy pseudobulbs with foliage 12 inches (30 cm) long, and they have a thick rooting system.

Zygopetalum (Zy-go-pet-a-lum)

From the Greek, referring to the base of the lip and the petals. Genus established in 1827. Twenty species known from South America. Modern hybrids are now being grown.

all about zygopetalums

In recent years, zygopetalums have become more popular as houseplants, but they are still not recommended as a first orchid. These compact plants, with their glossy green leaves, like cool temperatures.

These are cool to intermediate orchids, requiring a temperature range of 52°F (11°C) on winter nights to 86°F (30°C) in summer. They can be grown in most parts of the world, other than tropical climates. Where optimal temperatures can be maintained indoors, they are worth trying.

If the plant gets too cold, it may develop rot and fungal problems, which can appear as water-filled, warty patches on the pseudobulbs, or black marks on the foliage. Never spray the foliage. Instead, wipe the leaves regularly with a damp cloth to keep them free from dust.

The plant will have a resting period at some time during the winter, and this will vary according to the general growing conditions—for example, the amount of light and temperature levels. When resting and not in active growth, keep the plant a little dry until you see new growth. Do not let it become bone-dry, however. While the plants are in active growth, water them regularly, adding fertilizer at every other watering.

The green, sturdy flower spikes arise from the base of the new leaves when they are half grown and will grow clear of the foliage with little additional support. Each flower spike carries up to six or eight striking blooms 2 inches (5 cm) across. Leave the flowers on the plant until they wither, then cut the spike down at the base.

Do not take these orchids outdoors in summer, even in cool climates. Although they may look tough, their foliage is easily broken and can be damaged or marked by the wind and rain. They must never be placed in direct sun. In summer, they will grow indoors alongside cool-growing orchids such as odontoglossums. In winter, find a slightly warmer place for them; good light now will ensure that they bloom well the following spring.

REPOTTING ZYGOPETALUMS

Zygopetalums should be repotted regularly to accommodate their thick roots. Don't use too big a pot; put the plant directly in one only slightly larger, without disturbing its roots. After several years, you will need to strip out the root ball and cut away the dead roots, trimming the live ones back (see phragmipediums, pp. 78–9).

The plants freely produce more than one new growth each year, which means they can quickly double in size. Large plants may look majestic, with several flowering spikes in bloom at the same time, but they will take up a lot of room.

If space is limited, you can reduce their size by dividing them when repotting (see cymbidiums, pp. 44–5).

Zygopetalums are sold in various growing media. Some may do extremely well in Rockwool, others in the organic alternative of bark chips. When you repot your plant, do not mix the two types of growing medium. Instead, use the same type of compost it had when you bought it.

If you need to change the compost to fit in with other plants in your collection or because one type is harder to obtain than another, do this when you completely repot your plant. As you tease out the tangled roots, remove all traces of old compost. Plants that are moved from one compost to another will take time to adjust and may lose some of their leaves before settling down.

HELPFUL HINTS

SITE
Cool room indoors, with a minimum temperature of 52°F (11°C), away from direct sun.

OUTDOORS OR IN?
Never put outdoors, even in summer.

CARE
Keep watered all year round, but do not overwater. Wipe the leaves rather than spray the plant.

WHEN TO REPOT
Repot after several years, when the plant has outgrown the available space.

SIZE
Foliage on adult plants is 12 inches (30 cm) long. Blooms are up to 3 inches (7 cm) across.

Zygopetalum Everspring

New hybrids such as this striking clone
are being produced more readily now, as
the demand for these eye-catching
fragrant orchids grows.

Zygopetalum Artur Elle

A strong, robust modern hybrid that exhibits all of
the qualities you look for in a *Zygopetalum*. The
sepals and petals are rich chocolate brown with a
little of the green base color showing through. The
spreading white lip is heavily lined with purple,
which radiates from the center. The tall flower spikes
reach just above the foliage.

▼ Zygopetalum John Banks

In this handsome, sweetly scented hybrid, the basic green color of the sepals and petals is overlaid with nut brown bars. On the lip, it is almost totally obscured by the red staining.

Zygopetalum crinitum ▶

This species reveals the basic shape and coloring of the *Zygopetalum* and has contributed a lot to modern-day hybrids, including its sweet fragrance. The other illustrations in this chapter, all modern hybrids, have been bred from orchids like this one to produce bolder and better blooms.

other orchids

Most of the orchids in this book have gained popularity due to the beauty of their blooms and their amazing ability to thrive in the home. In addition to these long-established favorites, there are many more less well known orchids that can be grown alongside them. You are not likely to find many of the orchids on the following pages in your local garden center or store because they are not mass-produced, and you will need more skill—and sometimes special conditions—to grow them well. But not only do the orchids in this chapter give further insight into the remarkable diversity of orchids, they may also kindle your desire to learn more about these unique and extraordinary plants.

Commonly known as the Rag Orchid, *Coelogyne cristata* produces tumbling sprays of glistening white flowers with yellow centers.

all about vandas

Vandas love hot, humid conditions. In the wild, they grow in treetops near the equator—as far north as tropical China and as far south as Australia. Unless you live in a tropical climate, you will need to grow them in a specially adapted greenhouse, alongside other tropical plants.

In Singapore, vandas grow in profusion outdoors and appear to flower perpetually in the heat and humidity. Thousands can be found in commercial nurseries, growing in small wooden baskets hung from horizontal wires under awnings for protection from the tropical sun. The baskets hold no compost, only small pieces of charcoal for the plants' aerial roots to cling to and for retaining some moisture.

In the tropics, you can grow these orchids in a similar fashion, on a veranda or on garden trees. In a cool climate, vandas are best grown in a warm greenhouse or sunroom. They do not make successful houseplants because they need very high humidity, which is difficult to provide in the home and would be unpleasant for us to live in.

The way they grow

Vandas are monopodial orchids, meaning that they grow from a single stem. New leaves are continually produced from the top of the stem, growing alternately left and right and fanning out, while a mass of white aerial roots extends downward from the base. These roots can become extremely long; up to 3 feet (1 m) is not unusual. The plants continue to get taller as they get older and can reach 3 feet (1 m) within a few years. As they age, the older leaves are shed from the base, and in time the plant becomes leggy, with a length of bare stem below the foliage. To reduce their height, you can cut the plants down, severing the stem or central rhizome with a sharp knife or pruning shears. You must leave some aerial roots on the plant, otherwise it will shrivel, become dehydrated, and possibly die.

The stump that remains will often start to grow and within a few years will give you another plant of flowering size. Vandas sometimes produce side-shoots from the base of the plant; this is known as vegetative propagation.

Flowering

The flower spikes, which appear from the leaf axils on the stem, grow almost horizontally and bear up to eight large, flat blooms. The flowers have widely spread sepals and petals, which can be a single color or, most often, tessellated or mottled in rich hues. The lip is extremely small and inconspicuous. Blooms can vary from 2½ inches (6.5 cm) to 4 inches (10 cm) across, and flowering can occur at any time of the year.

Vanda (<u>Van</u>-da)

A Sanskrit word describing the way the plant grows. Genus established in 1795. Forty species known from Southeast Asia. Many hybrids are raised from seed, mostly in the tropics.

DO'S

✔ Tie the flower spike to a cane so that the heavy flowers do not pull the spike over and break it.

✔ Mist and feed with foliar feed regularly throughout the year. Spray frequently.

✔ Grow in semi-shade outdoors in tropical climates, in a warm greenhouse in a temperate climate.

✔ Provide plenty of light year round and shade from the hot midday sun.

DON'TS

✗ Do not grow in full sun.

✗ Do not allow to get too cold—below 64°F (18°C) on a winter's night.

✗ Do not allow to get too hot—over 90°F (32°C) in the summer.

✗ Do not repot.

GROWING VANDAS IN A GREENHOUSE

In temperate zones, vandas need to be grown in a greenhouse adapted for tropical conditions. For most of the year, you will need to provide some artificial heat in the greenhouse. Vandas require a minimum nighttime temperature of 64°F (18°C) both winter and summer, rising to a maximum during the day of 90°F (32°C). The high temperatures must be balanced by correspondingly high humidity, which can be achieved by spraying or misting several times a day. Feed the vandas regularly with foliar feed misted over the leaves and roots. They will not need repotting.

It is not as easy to provide the amount of light vandas require. They come from near the equator, so they are accustomed to 12 hours of daylight followed typically by 12 hours of darkness. In temperate regions, the longer summer days and shorter winter days create an imbalance for the plants; you may need to provide artificial light.

If a *Vanda* becomes too dry, the leaves crinkle as they dehydrate. This may be due to a lack of aerial roots. If this happens, spray more often and dip the plant several times daily in a bucket of water. Take care not to get water inside the tip where the new leaves come from or on the flowers; it will cause spotting. During the orchid's resting period, when the roots stop growing, continue to spray, but make sure that the plant is dry as the temperature drops toward nightfall.

Today, a wealth of hybrids, such as *Vascostylis (Vanda* x *Rynchostylis)* and *Ascocenda (Ascocentrum* x *Vanda)*, have been produced. It is within this group that the celebrated blue vandas, such as the hybrid *Vanda* Rothschildiana, are found. Their blooms are a color unlike any other in the orchid family. Other rainbow colors—deep purples, rich reds, brilliant oranges, and soft yellows—have been achieved by intensive selective breeding, which has also increased the size of the flowers.

Caring for vandas

Vandas sold in temperate climates have usually been bred and raised from seed in countries such as Thailand. When they are imported into their country of sale, they are strong and robust and often start to flower soon after arriving. This is the best time to buy plants.

When you get your *Vanda* home, it will probably have some dead roots. Cut these back, and they will sometimes regrow from near the stem of the plant. To give extra moisture, fill the basket with bark chips or a similar material to help compensate for the lack of humidity.

Although it is not practical to maintain a tropical greenhouse solely for a few vandas, you may consider having one if you want to grow a range of tropical plants. These might include climbers to provide shade during the summer.

Because of the damp conditions, most insect pests will not attack the vandas, but other plants can become infested with pests such as scale and mealybugs (see p.180), so you need to watch the vandas for signs of infestation.

Wild vandas are epiphytic, growing high in the forest trees. Their flowers look very different from the flowers of hybrids.

Ascocenda Thai Joy ▶

Tall, multi-flowered, upright flower spikes are the hallmark of this lovely bigeneric hybrid that displays its royal purple blooms with majestic pride.

◀ *Ascocenda* Princess Mikasa

This fine example shows the rich purple coloring and marbling effect on the sepals and petals of this popular variety. The flowers of ascocendas are slightly smaller than those of the true vandas, but they produce more blooms on a flower spike.

SITE
Give protection from sun and hang in a shaded area outdoors.

OUTDOORS OR IN?
Outdoors in the tropics. Indoors in cooler climates. Minimum temperature of 60°F (14°C).

CARE
Keep well sprayed all year. Add feed to water once a week.

WHEN TO REPOT
Do not repot.

SIZE
Adult plants can reach 3 feet (1 m) in height. Blooms are up to 4 inches (10 cm) across.

▲ *Vanda (Trudelia) cristata*

This attractive little flower, with its green sepals and petals and red embroidered lip, is a species from India that can be grown in a cool situation. Unlike the other vandas, it is suitable for indoor cultivation.

Vanda Kitty Blue ▶

Of all the vibrant colors found in the vandas, it is this deep indigo blue that represents all that is best about this genus. The flowers are heavily tessellated and the lip is darkest of all.

all about encyclias and coelogynes

These two popular genera contain many different and varied species. It is these species that are usually grown, rather than the few, mostly disappointing hybrids that have been produced.

Hybridizing has achieved little or no improvement on these two genera. Since there is only slight variation in the coloring of the species, it has proved impossible to produce different colored hybrids. Most plants sold in nurseries are species orchids grown from divisions of established stock or seed-raised plants.

Both encyclias and coelogynes produce plants ranging from only a few inches (centimeters) high to much larger specimens. They all have rounded or oval pseudobulbs, with a pair of narrow oval leaves.

Encyclias

These orchids usually bloom during the summer, producing a flower spike at the apex of the newly completed pseudobulb. Often a protective sheath encloses the buds in the early stage. Several flowers are carried on the flower spike, which will remain in bloom for three weeks or more. Many of the species are sweetly scented, and these bear white to creamy white flowers, often with delicate red markings on the lip.

One very fine exception to this usual coloring is *Encyclia vitellina*, whose 1-inch- (2.5-cm-) wide blooms are bright vermilion, with a lip tipped with orange-yellow. This plant is not as easy to grow as others in the genus, many of which will become large specimens more than 3 feet (1 m) across in a few years. Such a plant can be covered in hundreds of fragrant flowers. Since the plants produce several new growths each season, they do not take long to achieve such a large size. Divide them every three to four years to keep them at a size you can comfortably pick up and handle.

Coelogynes

The best-known coelogynes are the Indian species, which produce white or pale-colored flowers, varying from 1–2 inches (2.5–5 cm) across. Most of the species bloom in the spring and the flowers last for several weeks. The sepals and petals of the flowers of *Coelogyne cristata* var. *alba* have crimped edges, hence its common name of Rag Orchid.

The Cockleshell Orchid, *Encyclia cochleata,* is so called because of the shape of its lip, which is at the top of the flower.

Encyclia (En-sik-lee-ah)

From the Greek describing the way the lip encloses the column. The genus is related to cattleyas; established in 1828. One hundred and fifty species are known from the Americas. Species and a few hybrids are grown.

Coelogyne (See-law-ji-nee)

From the Greek meaning "hollow female," referring to a cavity in the stigma. Genus established in 1821. One hundred species are known from tropical Asia. Species and a few hybrids are grown.

A large plant will effervesce with tumbling blooms of the purest white on a pendant flower spike.

The Malaysian species are quite distinct from those from India. They are often much larger, with tall, oval, upright leaves. Large green flowers are prominent, with others that are off-white. A few notable hybrids have been produced from these species. For most homes, the Indian species are a better choice, since they are smaller—most will fit easily on a windowsill—and bloom reliably.

Caring for encyclias and coelogynes

Both genera are cool-growing orchids and need the same care. At night, keep them at a temperature of around 50°F (10°C) and by day no higher than 80°F (27°C). They will do well alongside odontoglossums, since they also need plenty of light and fresh air all year round.

These orchids have a resting period during the winter, when they need little water. In the spring, the flower spikes protrude from the new growths and produce their flowers close to the foliage.

The dainty flowers of *Encyclia nemorale* appear at the end of a long flower spike.

After flowering, keep the plants watered and fed until the end of the growing season. Spray them lightly during the summer. Repot after two years if the pot is overcrowded, keeping the plant in as small a pot as possible.

DO'S

✔ Water during the growing period and feed at every second or third watering.

✔ Grow on a cool, well-lit windowsill.

✔ Repot after flowering when necessary. Divide every three to four years if desired to keep to a manageable size.

DON'TS

✘ Do not grow in full sun.

✘ Do not spray the leaves too heavily.

✘ Do not overwater during the resting period.

✘ Do not allow to get too cold—below 50°F (10°C) on a winter's night.

✘ Do not allow to get too hot—over 80°F (27°C).

The flower spikes of *Coelogyne intermedia* form glorious sprays of golden-centered white flowers.

Encyclia cochleata ▶

This charming orchid has the lip at the top of the flower rather than at the bottom as in so many other orchids. It resembles a cockleshell, hence its common name of Cockleshell Orchid.

Coelogyne speciosa ▼

This Malaysian species produces large flowers in succession over a long period in summer. Some varieties have different colored lips as seen here, with dark orange (left) and peach (right) being the most common.

HELPFUL HINTS

SITE
Grow in a cool room, out of the sun.

OUTDOORS OR IN?
Indoors all year round.

CARE
Water well in the summer; less in the winter. Add feed once a week.

WHEN TO REPOT
Every two to three years.

SIZE
Adult plants can reach 12 inches (30 cm) in height. Blooms are up to 2 inches (5 cm) across.

all about pleiones

These orchids develop rapidly and complete their pseudobulbs during a single summer, so they give quick results. Some of the modern hybrids are more robust and easier to rear than the species, but they can be harder to find and are often more expensive.

P leiones are seasonal orchids, used to living in an environment that has both a wet and a dry season. In the spring, the plants start their new growth from the base of the previous season's pseudobulb. When the growth is a few inches (centimeters) high, a single bud (occasionally two) emerges from inside the growth on a short stem. The 3-inch- (7-cm-) wide flower opens to reveal narrow, sparkling sepals and petals surrounding a trumpet-shaped, frilled lip. In the species, the color range is restricted to pink, white, and yellow.

Recent hybridizing has broadened this range to include many shades of pink, bordering on an elusive peach, and darkening almost to red, as well as pure white and buttery yellow. The lips, too, are varied, with pink, red, and orange stripes and veining. The blooms last for about ten days.

The cycle of growth

After flowering, the new growth continues upward, forming a single, narrow, oval ribbed leaf, which is light green and about 6 inches (15 cm) high. The base of the new growth swells out into a squat or rounded pseudobulb, which is dark green to purple, depending upon the color of the flower.

Growth is completed by the end of the summer, by which time the plant enters its winter rest. The solitary leaf turns yellow, often becoming spotted with age before being shed, and the plant remains dormant until spring. In its natural habitat, this ensures that the orchid can survive extremely cold winters, when the pseudobulbs are often covered in snow for much of the time.

Pleione pseudobulbs are short-lived and wither and die in only their second year, but a single pseudobulb will often produce two new growths at the same time, doubling the number of pseudobulbs for the next season. In this way, several pseudobulbs will result from a single one within a few years. The best way to display these orchids is to grow several together in a shallow pot. One large pot containing a dozen or more blooms is far more impressive than several pots with just one or two flowers at a time.

The right growing conditions

Pleiones are very cool-growing orchids and will not do well in warmer climates. When grown in temperate areas, they thrive indoors with little

The masses of flowers on *Pleione* El Pico Gold Crest certainly grab the attention. The blooms are vibrant pink with intense coloring on the lips and rich, glowing markings.

Pleione (Play-<u>oh</u>-nee)

Common name Crocus Orchid. The name derives from the star cluster known as the Pleiades. Genus established in 1825. Sixteen species from India to China. Both species and hybrids are grown.

POTTING PLEIONES

Pleiones overwinter as single, leafless pseudobulbs. They remain dormant until the spring, when they should be potted (see right). After potting, water the plant carefully until it has made new roots. Choose a large pseudobulb if you want it to flower that year; a small one will make only new growth.

By the end of the growing season, older pseudobulbs often produce tiny bulbils around the top. These can be cut off and carefully potted in the spring. They will grow, forming small pseudobulbs. By the following year, these will produce larger pseudobulbs that will be strong enough to produce a flowering growth the next spring.

In spring, new growths begin to appear on the old pseudobulbs. This is the time to pot them.

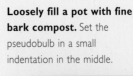

Loosely fill a pot with fine bark compost. Set the pseudobulb in a small indentation in the middle.

Six weeks later, after flowering, roots and one large leaf have grown.

heat. During the winter, while they are dormant, they require a frost-free position; in sheltered places, they can remain outdoors all year round. A good solution is to place the pot of plants outside for the summer, returning it to a frost-free position with plenty of light indoors for the winter.

These little orchids do best where they will get plenty of air and light, and they must be kept moist. These conditions will produce hardened and ripened pseudobulbs that will bloom well the following spring. If conditions indoors are too warm, the plants will produce a taller, paler leaf that is lush and floppy. The pseudobulb will be smaller than it should be, and the plant is unlikely to bloom the following spring.

Caring for pleiones

Pleiones can be obtained from a specialist nursery at any time of the year—established in their pots and in various stages of growth. Dormant pseudobulbs are also available in early spring in polyethylene bags, with the compost in which to pot them. Pot them immediately and keep them

lightly watered until the new growth appears. Gradually increase watering to encourage the new roots, which start to grow at about the same time.

After flowering, lift out the old, flowered stem from the center of the new growth; this will not harm the plant. Keep the plants evenly watered and give a half-strength feed every third watering. When the early morning frosts are over, place the pot outdoors in a sheltered spot where it will be shaded from midday sun. Half-burying a pot in the soil will help keep the plants cooler at the base. Keep slugs and snails away from the developing growths and protect the plants from rodents.

When the plants have shed their leaves, bring them indoors for the winter. Store them in a cool dry place that has plenty of light and is frost free. You can either leave the plants until spring or take them out of the pot, retaining only the fresh, green pseudobulbs, which will remain plump all winter without any moisture. Cut back any dead roots to about 1 inch (2.5 cm) and lay the pseudobulbs in a seed tray. When you pot the orchids in the spring, the old roots will anchor them in the new pot.

DO'S
✔ Water throughout the growing season and feed at half-strength every third watering.

✔ Grow outdoors in a cool location in the summer.

✔ In a sheltered site, leave plants outdoors in winter. In a temperate climate, keep dormant plants in a cool, frost-free position with plenty of light indoors.

✔ Repot pseudobulbs in the spring.

DON'TS
✗ Do not grow in a warm place.

✗ Do not water plants when they are dormant in winter.

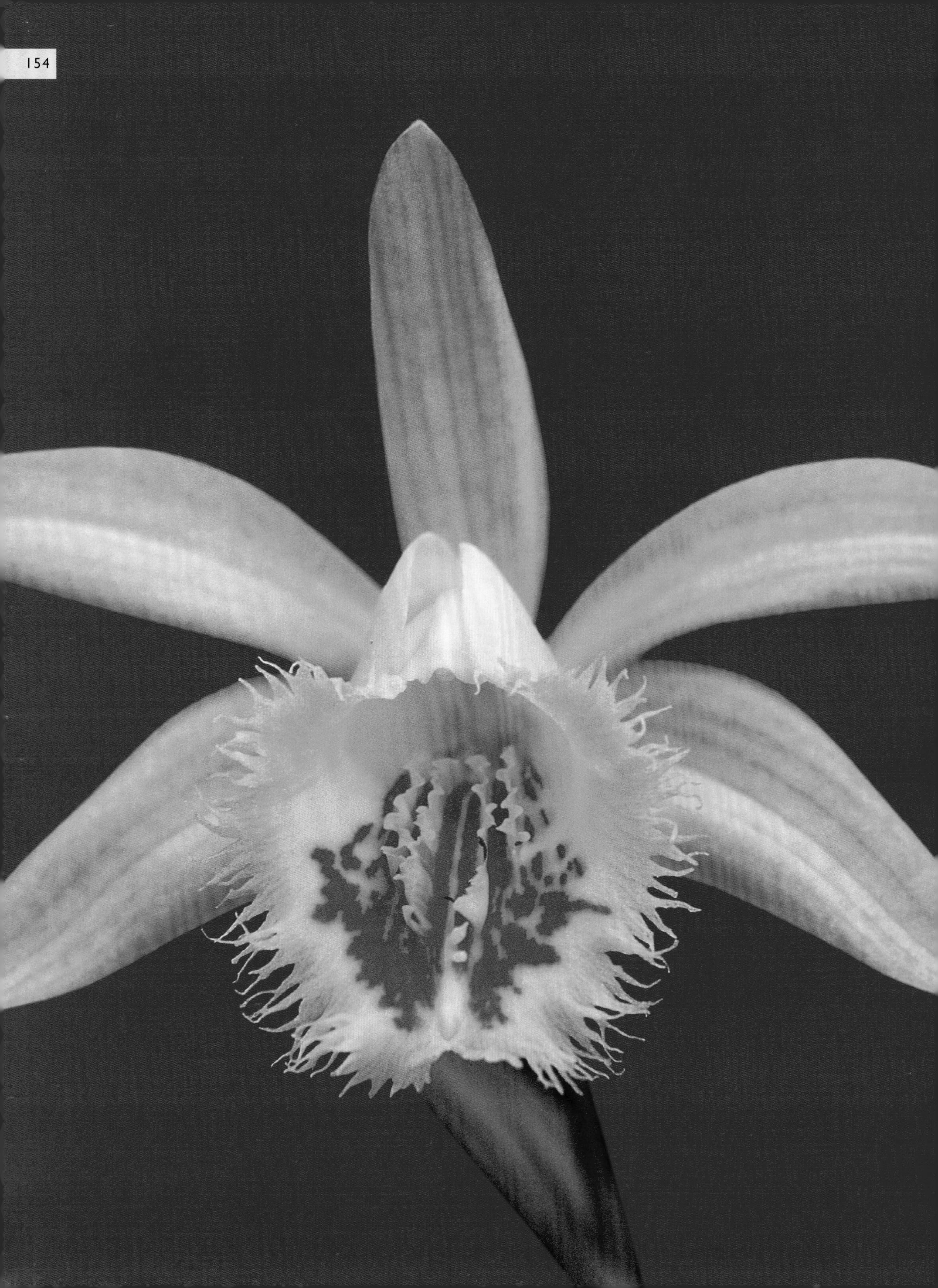

SITE
Cool room
indoors, away from
direct sun.

OUTDOORS OR IN?
Outdoors in
summer and winter
(if above freezing).

CARE
Keep watered all
summer. Leave dry
in winter.

WHEN TO REPOT
Repot when
new growth
shows.

SIZE
Adult plants are
9 inches (23 cm)
high and across.
Blooms are
3 inches (7 cm)
or more across.

◄ *Pleione* Shantung 'Ridgeway'

This outstanding hybrid was given an Award of Merit by
Britain's Royal Horticultural Society for its unusual coloring.
It has peach-colored sepals and petals with a contrasting
yellow lip decorated at its center with crimson red.

▼ *Pleione* Versailles

An extremely popular and robust hybrid that
can produce two flowers on a single stem. The
flowers have mauve-pink sepals and petals; the
outstanding lip is marked with deep blood red.

all about lycastes

In the wild, Lycaste species can be epiphytic, lithophytic, or terrestrial; all grow in shady places. The smaller species and some hybrids are best for indoor growing, since some of the hybrids can become extremely large.

These are seasonal orchids, with a clearly marked summer growing season followed by a dormant period during the winter, when they can withstand dry conditions.

The robust plants produce plump, oval, dark green pseudobulbs topped by a few large, broad, ribbed leaves. These are softly textured, lasting for one or two years at the most. Usually, only one season's pseudobulbs are in leaf on a plant at any one time. With lycastes, if more pseudobulbs are out of leaf than in leaf, the plant is not considered by growers to be unbalanced, as it would be in a *Cymbidium* or *Odontoglossum*.

Flowering

The flower spikes appear in the spring at about the same time as the new growths, which soon fan out into leaves, while the flower spikes continue to grow to a few inches (centimetres) tall, each with a single bud. The blooms are typically three-cornered in shape; the triangle is formed by the sepals, which are set wide apart. The petals and lip, which are

Lycaste (Lye-kass-tee)

Named for Helen of Troy's sister. Genus established in 1843. Forty-nine species from the forests of Central and South America to Bolivia. Both species and hybrids are grown.

about the same size, point forward to form a triangle at the center of the flower. A healthy plant will produce many flowers from one pseudobulb.

Colors found in the species include white, brown, and green, as well as pink, as in *Lycaste skinneri,* or yellow, as in *L. aromatica.* This latter, green-gold species is beautifully fragrant. Among the hybrids, there are many more colors.

After flowering, the plants grow rapidly during the summer and all growth is completed by winter. This is their resting period. Some lycastes will shed their foliage at this time, remaining in a deciduous state for the winter; others discard their aging foliage only when new growth starts in spring.

Related species

Closely related to the lycastes are the anguloas, or Tulip Orchids—their big waxy blooms are cupped, like a tulip. These are even larger-growing plants of similar appearance, which, when crossed with lycastes, produce the handsome angulocastes. There are many variations in their shape and color—often they are spotted and speckled, with a fragrance carried through from one species, *Anguloa clowesii.*

The right conditions

Orchids such as lycastes, which have a short, fast growing season, need all the help they can get to

DO'S

✔ Water during the growing period and feed at every second or third watering. Water sparingly in winter when the plant is resting.

✔ Grow in the shade on a warm windowsill and provide high humidity.

✔ Repot every year in the spring. Remove the oldest pseudobulbs.

✔ Divide the plant when repotting if necessary.

✔ Tie the flower spike to a cane when the plant is in bloom so that the flowers do not droop.

DON'TS

✘ Do not grow in full sun.

✘ Do not spray the leaves too heavily; water lodging in the crown can spot the leaves.

✘ Do not allow to get too cold—below 60°F (16°C) on a winter's night.

✘ Do not allow to get too hot—over 85°F (30°C).

develop and mature before winter. Giving them plenty of water and keeping temperatures high will improve their growing conditions.

While they are growing, lycastes need shade and plenty of space in which their large, spreading leaves can develop. They grow rapidly, and do best in temperatures no higher than 85°F (30°C) during the summer. They need a nighttime temperature no lower than 60°F (16°C) in the winter.

Higher temperatures mean that the humidity should also be high. Put a tray with water below the plants and lightly mist the foliage early in the day so that the leaves have dried off before the temperature begins to drop toward the evening.

Summer care

Summertime gives the plant the opportunity to complete its pseudobulbs, which should be the same size as the previous ones, or larger. If the pseudobulbs get smaller each year, this will affect the plant's flowering, as well as future growth. A succession of smaller pseudobulbs can indicate a problem such as dryness over a long period, or temperatures that are too low.

Repotting lycastes

These strong growers quickly fill their pots, so you should repot them every year, just after flowering (see odontoglossums, p. 61). This encourages them to produce good-sized pseudobulbs each season. By removing the oldest pseudobulbs, the plants can often be returned to the same size pot. Pot the older pseudobulbs individually, and provided they are still green and plump, they will produce new growths of their own. Within two to three years, you will have another plant that will bloom for you.

You can also split up the plants into smaller divisions. Do this in the spring before the new growths have started. With fewer older pseudobulbs, the plants have a better chance of producing new growth and achieving another peak.

The tuliplike flowers of *Anguloa clowesii* rise from the new growth in spring. They are bright yellow and sweetly scented.

CARING FOR LYCASTES

During the winter, while lycastes are resting, they need to be kept cool, with as much light as possible. Keep the large pseudobulbs plump by watering occasionally. If the leaves have become yellow or spotted with age, cut them off: they are no longer helping the plant. Without their leaves, the plants take up less space and can be placed close together.

In spring, new growths and flower spikes will emerge, surrounding the latest pseudobulbs. Give the plants water in moderation, taking care not to get water inside the developing new growths or on the buds.

The flower spike of some lycastes plants will be weighed down by the heavy flower as it matures, and it may need to be tied upright to a small cane. After flowering is over, begin feeding the plants at every second or third watering, depending on how rapidly they are growing.

SITE
Warm room indoors, away from direct sun.

OUTDOORS OR IN?
Do not put outdoors, even in summer.

CARE
Water well in the summer; sparingly in the winter.

WHEN TO REPOT
Repot every year in the spring. Remove the old pseudobulbs. Divide the plant if necessary.

SIZE
Adult plants are up to 2 feet (60 cm) high and across. Blooms are 3 inches (7 cm) or more across.

▼ *Lycaste* Betty Sparrow

This attractive flower is a pale primrose yellow. Its sepals are generous and fleshy. The single blooms are heavy, so they will need to be supported with a stake.

Lycaste Always x Auburn ▶

A new, as yet unnamed hybrid, showing the typical three-cornered shape. Its contrasting coloring shows strong pink sepals with lighter petals and a red lip.

all about masdevallias

Masdevallias are fun to grow—their cheery blooms will brighten any home, and despite their reputation for being difficult, the modern hybrids are fascinating and rewarding orchids.

These orchids do best in cooler climates, where they will grow well in a cool, airy atmosphere. They are not suited to tropical conditions and cannot withstand temperatures above 80°F (27°C).

Precious and rare

Although this is a large genus, many of the species are extremely rare today. Masdevallias are not suitable for meristem culture and are propagated from seed or by division. Hybrids, bred mainly in the U.S., are becoming more plentiful. As the cultural requirements of these orchids are better understood, their popularity is increasing. The modern hybrids can be grown indoors with considerable success, but the rare species belong in the collections of serious collectors. These plants are precious and must not be lost by carelessness or inexperience—the hybrids are more expendable and therefore more suitable for most people.

Masdevallia (Maz-de-vah-lee-ah)

Common name Kite Orchid. Named for the Spanish botanist Dr. José Masdevall. Genus established in 1794. Three hundred and forty species, many rare, are known from South America. Both species and hybrids are grown.

The cycle of growth

Masdevallias produce short stems topped by a single, often brittle, narrow oval leaf. The foliage forms tufts, and the orchids quickly develop into large mature plants.

Mainly summer flowering, the flower spikes on masdevallias arise from the base of the leading growths. Depending upon the variety, these may be short—4–6 inches (10–15 cm) long—or up to about 14 inches (36 cm). Those with short spikes leave their blooms nodding over the rim of the pot, while the taller-growing types stand upright. They may need to be staked.

Brightly colored blooms

The blooms come in a huge variety of colors and patterns, including vibrant orange and light yellow, and are often striped or speckled. The most popular plants have blood-red, moon-shaped single blooms on a tall stem.

Although some of the flowers are trumpet shaped and do not open fully, all masdevallias conform to the same basic design, with large, oversized sepals. The sepals are the plant's main attraction and are fused partway along their length. They are cupped at the base, where the extremely small, insignificant petals and lip can be seen forming a tiny triangle. In the most dramatic flowers, the sepals end in long tails, giving rise to the plant's common name of Kite Orchid.

During the summer, masdevallias can remain in bloom for a few weeks, although all the flowers will not be open at the same time. The plants that produce the tallest flower spikes need to be supported with canes.

Caring for masdevallias

These epiphytic plants grow in the wild in shaded tree canopies in mountainous areas of South America. To mimic conditions in their mountain home, you will need to find a cool place for them where temperatures will never get too high. They need a temperature of 45–55°F (7–13°C) on winter nights and not above about 75°F (24°C) in the summer. Masdevallias need to be kept in light shade throughout the year, since too much light, particularly in summer, can cause yellowing or spotting of the foliage.

The right pot

Grow masdevallias in as small a pot as possible. Small plastic basket pots of the type used for aquatic plants are ideal since they allow the air to flow around their fine roots. The roots will grow through the mesh pots and sometimes the plants themselves will protrude through the pot. Always use a fine grade of fir bark for potting.

These orchids dislike disturbance and should be divided only when it is absolutely necessary. Divide them into large pieces.

Humidity and watering

High humidity and airy conditions are the key to growing masdevallias well. They do not have pseudobulbs and do not rest in winter, so you will need to make sure that the plants remain evenly moist throughout the year, without ever becoming too wet or drying out completely. Overwatering will quickly lead to loss of foliage, and once rot gets into a plant, it is difficult to solve the resulting problems (see p.179).

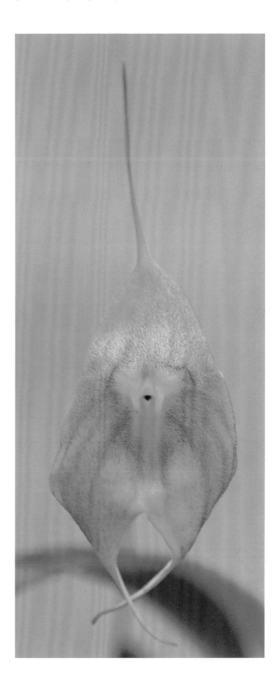

Masdevallia **Inca Prince** has a stunning orange flower, streaked with red at the center.

DO'S

✓ Water throughout the year and feed at every second or third watering. Maintain high humidity.

✓ Grow in light shade on a cool windowsill or in the center of a room.

✓ Repot after flowering only when the plant outgrows its pot. Divide only when absolutely necessary.

✓ Tie a long flower spike to a cane when the plant is in bloom so that the weight of the flowers does not snap the spike.

DON'TS

✗ Do not grow in full sun.

✗ Do not spray the leaves too heavily.

✗ Do not allow to get too cold—below 45°F (7°C) on a winter's night.

✗ Do not allow to get too hot—over 75°F (24°C).

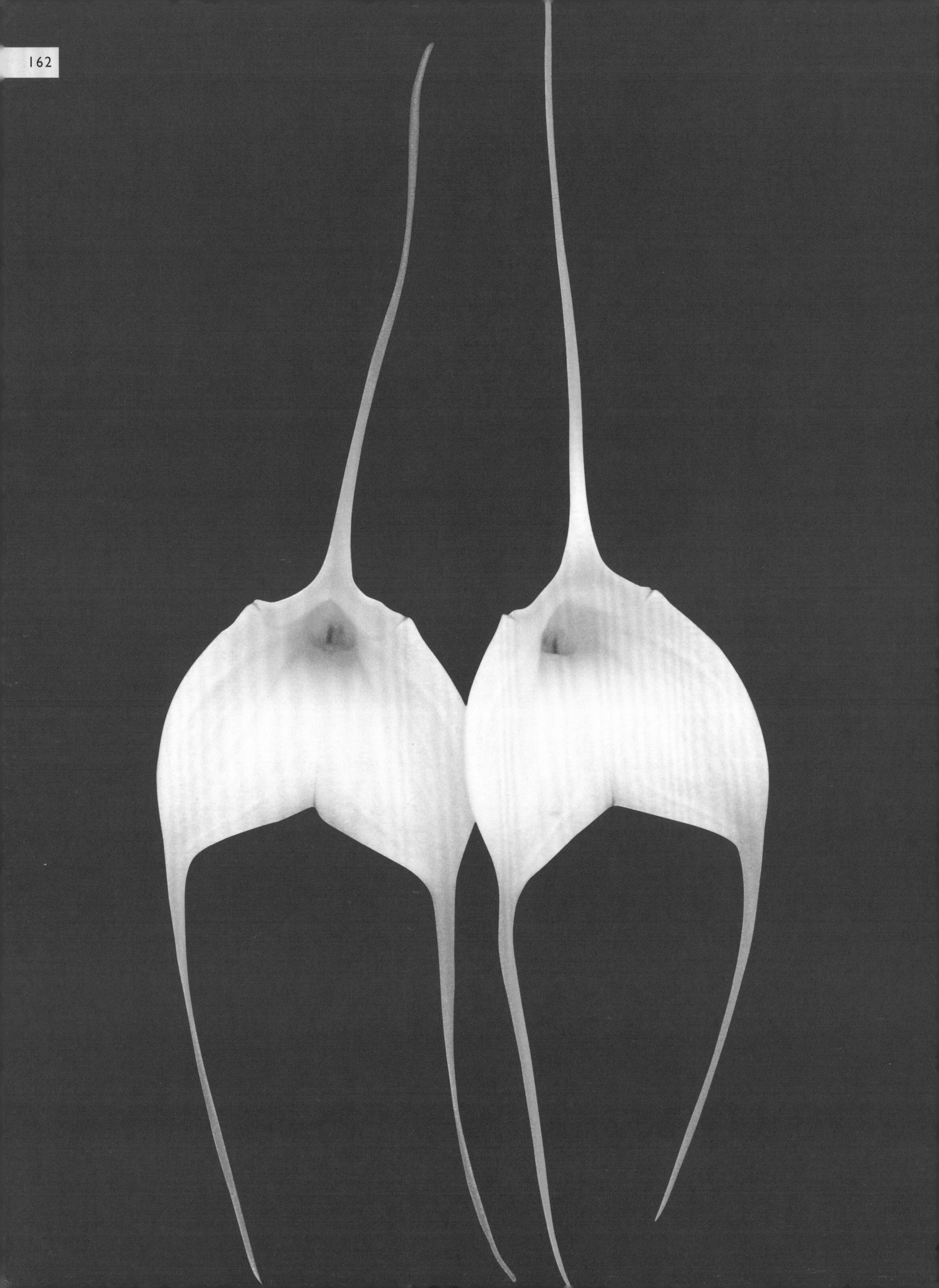

HELPFUL HINTS

SITE
Cool, shaded
windowsill, away
from direct sun.

OUTDOORS OR IN?
Do not put
outdoors, even
in summer.

CARE
Keep watered all
year round, but do
not overwater.

WHEN TO REPOT
Repot after
flowering, only when
the plant outgrows
its pot.

SIZE
Adult plants can
reach 14 inches
(36 cm) high.
Blooms are 3 inches
(7 cm) or more
across.

◄ *Masdevallia* Bella Donna x *M. urosalpinx*

From tall, slender stems come these
ghostly pale, creamy yellow flowers, their
tails standing out in burnt orange.

Masdevallia Magdalena x Marguerite ►

The exquisitely colored blooms of this
newly produced hybrid shine with glowing
orange overlaid with crimson. The sepals
are fused to form a rounded moon shape
that encircles the small petals and lip.

displaying orchids

Orchids lend themselves to imaginative methods of display. The purity of their colors, from brilliant white to luminous pinks and yellows and the darkest crimsons, makes them stand out in any room. You can use them to decorate a dinner table for a formal party or to add a welcoming touch to a hallway. Wherever you display your orchids, they are sure to give you pleasure with every glance and to attract the admiration of visitors.

A stunning combination of light and color is created by floating individual cut blooms and floating candles in a shallow glass bowl.

displaying your blooms

Make the most of your orchids when they are in bloom by showing them off in a part of the house where you and your visitors can see them.

Phalaenopsis blooms
look stunning floating
above a leafy fern base.

Contrasting flowers
can be grouped together
for a colorful effect.

Most orchids will remain in bloom for several weeks. During this time, you will want to display them to their best advantage. This may mean removing them from their normal position if it is in a part of the house where visitors are unlikely to go, and placing them in the center of your dining room table or in your living room where they can be admired by all. While on display, stake your orchids so that their blooms will look their best.

With multi-flowered orchids such as cymbidiums, phalaenopsis, and odontoglossums, wait until most of the blooms on the flower spikes are open before moving them out of their normal quarters and into your display area. If you move them too soon— while they are still in tight bud—the change in light and possibly other factors can cause the buds to turn yellow and drop off (see bud blast, p. 176).

Preparing your orchids

Before putting your orchids on display, clean the leaves by wiping them with a damp cloth. Never use leaf shine sprays on orchids because it clogs the leaves. Water the plants thoroughly and allow them to drain. You can cover the top of the compost with moss or pebbles if you wish, but remove this decorative touch whenever you water the plants. Finally, check around the flowers and look under the leaves for aphids and other pests such as mealybugs

AFTER FLOWERING

As soon as the blooms have finished, cut off the old flower spike and remove the stake used to support it. If you have moved the plant, return it to its normal growing position. Check to make sure that the plant is wet enough. It may have dried out while on display. If it is too dry, water it thoroughly. You should also check the plant for aphids and other pests such as mealybugs or scale insects (see p. 180).

and scale insects. You want to display only healthy, bug-free plants. If you find an outbreak of bugs, you will need to treat it before displaying your orchids (see pp. 180–181).

Grouping orchids

If you have more than one orchid in bloom at a time, you can show them off by grouping them together in a pebble tray. Fill a tray large enough to fit all the orchids with pebbles and add water, making sure that the water level is below the pebbles. Finally, place your orchids on the moist pebbles. Pots of small ferns mixed in with the orchids add both humidity and attractive foliage.

Orchids can also be displayed in a row on a windowsill. Be sure that the sunlight is not too bright for the particular genus and that no part of the orchid touches the glass where the sun's heat could burn the plant.

DO'S
✓ Keep the plants watered while they are on display.

✓ Remove any decorative moss or pebbles from the surface of the pot when you return the plants to their growing area.

✓ Check for aphids and other pests.

DON'TS
✗ Do not keep dead or dying blooms in the display. Cut off flowers from the bottom of the spike as they die.

✗ Do not spray the blooms with water. It will mark them.

✗ Do not allow the orchids to get hotter or colder than recommended.

MAKING A DISPLAY CABINET

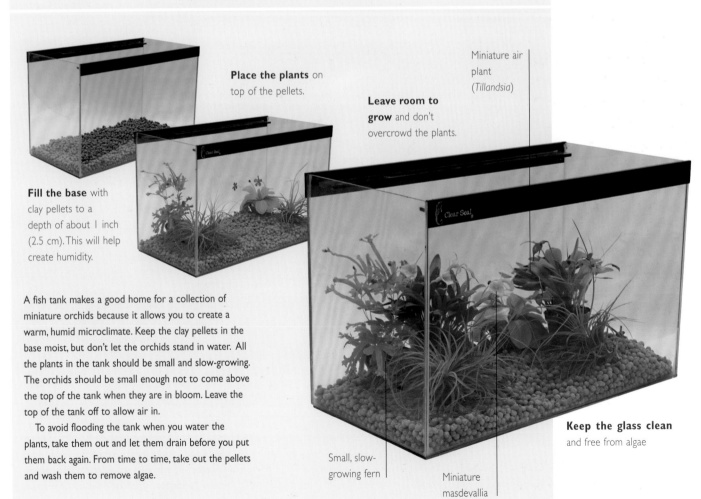

Fill the base with clay pellets to a depth of about 1 inch (2.5 cm). This will help create humidity.

Place the plants on top of the pellets.

Leave room to grow and don't overcrowd the plants.

Miniature air plant (*Tillandsia*)

Keep the glass clean and free from algae

Small, slow-growing fern

Miniature masdevallia

A fish tank makes a good home for a collection of miniature orchids because it allows you to create a warm, humid microclimate. Keep the clay pellets in the base moist, but don't let the orchids stand in water. All the plants in the tank should be small and slow-growing. The orchids should be small enough not to come above the top of the tank when they are in bloom. Leave the top of the tank off to allow air in.

To avoid flooding the tank when you water the plants, take them out and let them drain before you put them back again. From time to time, take out the pellets and wash them to remove algae.

mounting on bark

Growing orchids on bark can be a great way to enjoy them. It is closest to the way they live in their natural state.

Not all orchids are suitable for growing on bark. The smaller epiphytic type that would be found growing on trees in nature is the best choice. These orchids string out their pseudobulbs along a continually extending rhizome, or stem. Such plants grow quickly over the edge of the pot, adopting an upward or horizontal mode of growing. Other

Orchids with long flower spikes grow well on bark.

plants may be intent on growing downward. These plants grow well on bark.

Orchids growing on bark will dry out faster than orchids in pots. Spray them or dip them in water every day to keep them moist. Unless you are vigilant about this, they will dry out in the home. Ideally, orchids mounted on bark should be kept in a greenhouse or display case.

MOUNTING AN ORCHID ON BARK

YOU WILL NEED:
◆ Tree fern, coconut fiber, or other material that is slow to decompose
◆ *Sphagnum* moss
◆ A piece of cork bark
◆ A suitable mature orchid in need of repotting
◆ Garden wire
◆ Craft knife or pruning shears and pliers

Position the plant on the rough side of the bark. Any new growths should point upward. Secure with wire and use pliers to tighten. Repeat so the plant stays in place. Attach a piece of wire to the bark so that you can hang it up later.

3

1

Remove the plant from its pot. Shake out the old compost from between the roots. Prune the roots and remove any old pseudobulbs.

Sandwich the orchid between the *Sphagnum* moss and the tree fern or coconut fiber to surround it on all sides.

2

4

Trim the moss and fiber so that they look neat, not straggly. They will help the plant stay moist and form new roots.

Dip the plant in water. Leave it submerged for ten minutes so that it gets a thorough soaking.

5

Well-established in its hanging basket, this *Brassia* is a delightful specimen.

hanging gardens

Many orchids adapt well to growing in a basket. You can buy a suitable container or make your own slatted wooden basket.

In order to grow orchids in baskets, you need to suspend them where you can water them *in situ*. It is a chore to take them down for watering; if they are large and heavy, it may be almost impossible. In either case, the result will be that the plant is not watered frequently enough.

In tropical regions, hang your basket of orchids from a tree in the garden—excess water will drain onto the ground. In cooler climates, a sunroom with a tiled floor is a good place to hang a large basket of orchids. The water that drains out after watering can be easily mopped up. Indoors, use small baskets. They are easier to take down for watering, but the orchids will need almost daily dipping to stop them from drying out.

ORCHIDS FOR BASKETS

Brassias have long drooping flower spikes that can be left unsupported.

Coelogyne cristata can grow very big, forming a huge mound of pseudobulbs.

Choose dendrobiums with drooping canes such as this *D. parishii*.

Encyclias, like this plant of *E. nemorale*, produce pendant flower spikes that look lovely trailing from a basket.

Most vandas do well in baskets because of their long aerial roots.

Dendrobium parishii produces drooping canes that make it ideal for growing in a basket.

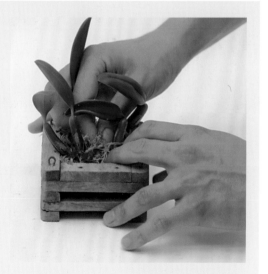

This epiphytic orchid will grow to form a complete ball around the basket.

PLANTING INTO A BASKET

It is often possible to slip an orchid from its pot and drop it into a basket of the same size with its root ball intact. If it is not possible or if, as here, you are potting a piece of a larger plant, you will need to repot using *Sphagnum* moss. Use the smallest basket you can—the plant will grow over and around it. There is also less risk of overwatering. Make sure that you have tucked the plant firmly in place before attaching string or wire to the top of the basket. Hang it in a place where you can reach it easily, since you will need to water the plant frequently, particularly if the basket is small.

You will need an orchid, a slatted basket, and moss. The *Sphagnum* moss will not fall through the bars.

Place the orchid in the basket with the moss. Tuck it in firmly with your fingertips.

orchids at night

Orchids can look fantastic under artificial lighting. After dark, give your orchids a luminous glow to really show off their blooms. If you are using candles, votives, or fairy lights, remember that they give off heat as well as light and can damage your orchids. Check that the plants are not getting too hot by holding your hand near them—if your hand feels hot, move the light source away.

▼ **A trio of pure white phalaenopsis plants** completes this black and white table setting for a formal dinner.

▲ **Sparkling fairy lights** have been wired up the stake holding up the flower spike to accent this orchid's lovely pale mauve blooms.

Candles and votives ▶ look lovely, but do not place them too close to the orchids or keep them burning too long. They generate heat as well as light and can damage the flowers and foliage.

problem solving

Orchids can live in cultivation for many years—up to 100 years in established botanical gardens, for example. But for this to happen, growing conditions have to be right and any problems must be dealt with promptly. This chapter covers the most common major problems, tells you how to spot them, and what to do about them. Over time, orchids progress in peaks and valleys. They advance toward a peak, producing optimum growth and flowers. Then they may regress and take some time before achieving another high performance crest. By recognizing these progressions in your orchids, you will be able to encourage them to grow and flower for years to come.

Ladybug (Ladybird Beetle)

Small, round, carnivorous flying insect. Brightly colored, usually red or yellow with black spots. Loved by orchid growers because they eat aphids and other pests.

problems with blooms

The buds and flowers, the softest parts of an orchid, are most susceptible to problems within the environment where the orchid is growing.

Non-flowering, pseudobulbs

Description Plants are healthy, producing foliage from new pseudobulbs, but no flower spikes. Affects cymbidiums and other orchids that have pseudobulbs.

Causes Each year, the pseudobulbs on an orchid should become larger until the maximum size is reached. By this time, the plant will be of flowering size and a flower spike will be produced. If the pseudobulbs are getting smaller, the orchids will not flower. The reason for this may be that too many of the older pseudobulbs have shed their foliage.

Cure Repot the orchid and at the same time remove the older, leafless pseudobulbs to restore the balance of the plant. With fewer pseudobulbs to support, the plant can grow forward again. When larger pseudobulbs are produced, flower spikes will follow.

Non-flowering, other types

Description Plants are healthy, producing plenty of foliage but no flower spikes.

Causes *Cool-growing orchids* These may not flower if the temperatures are too high. They will then produce lush growth and no flowers. *Warmer-growing orchids* If these are grown in conditions that are too warm, they will have dark green, limp foliage and no flowers.

Cure *Cool-growing orchids* Move plants to cooler surroundings. In time, they should start to flower again.
Warmer-growing orchids Phalaenopsis may need a 2–3 week period of cooler nighttime temperatures to initiate flowering. Only do this when a healthy plant has not produced the expected flower spike for several months.

Bud blast

Description All of the buds that have been developing normally on the flowering spike turn yellow and drop off, just as they are about to open.

Causes The causes of bud blast can include overwatering, cold and wet conditions, or, at the other extreme, surroundings that are too warm and dry. A stuffy, poorly ventilated atmosphere will also cause buds to fall off.

Cure Try to maintain the correct growing conditions for your orchids. If a plant is ready to flower, do not change the conditions by, for instance, bringing it indoors from a greenhouse or moving it around the room. Instead, wait until the flowers are fully open before moving the plant.

Flower-wilt

Description Flowers wilt prematurely, even though orchid blooms can be expected to last for several weeks.

Causes The reason for flower-wilt can often be overheating or overdryness. Flower-wilt often occurs in recently purchased orchids that have been left in their cellophane wrappers for too long before being sold.

Cure Prevention rather than cure is the answer here. Choose only healthy plants when buying, and remove an orchid from any wrapping as soon as you get it home. Pay careful attention to the growing conditions needed for different orchids, and try to provide an environment as close as possible to the ideal.

Red lips

Description This is most often seen on cymbidiums, where the flowers have either become aged or have lost their pollen. The lips turn red and the flower dies.

Causes Pollen can be dislodged due to rough handling. On plants outdoors, it may be eaten by mice or pecked off by small birds. Once the pollen has been removed, the flower dies. If the pollen has already turned black, it has rotted, and the bloom will soon wither and die.

Cure Handle plants carefully to avoid damaging them. Outdoors, prevention is the only cure—try to make sure that the plants are not vulnerable to raiding animals.

Spotting

Description Blooms will often become spotted as they age, but spotting that occurs while the flowers are still fresh is caused by a fungal disease called botrytis. It is most often seen on cattleya and phalaenopsis blooms.

Causes Cold and damp conditions or a lack of ventilation will encourage the development of the fungus. It is most common in winter when temperatures are lowest.

Cure Destroy infected flowers and isolate any plants that are infected so that the fungus does not spread. Give careful attention to the conditions in which your orchids are growing. Increase the air flow around the plants and reduce humidity to help to prevent the incidence of botrytis.

problems with foliage

An orchid should have firm, medium-green leaves.
If it doesn't, check for the problems covered here.

Black marks

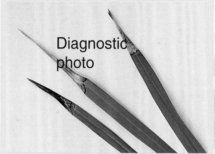
Diagnostic photo

Description Black or brown markings or spots form on the leaves. The tips of the leaves can also be affected. The black starts at the tip and runs down the leaf.

Cause Sometimes spotted leaves do not indicate a problem. When they are old, leaves may develop spots before turning yellow and being discarded by the plant in the natural cycle of growth. Black tips that appear on older leaves are part of the aging process. If young leaves have black tips, this is most probably caused by overwatering or by nighttime temperatures that are too low.

Cure Sometimes the infection can be stopped by cutting off the diseased part of the leaf. Check the roots to see whether the plant has been overwatered. Repot if necessary, or increase the temperatures. (Look at the appropriate chapter to find out what those are.) If the cause is a fungal infection, an anti-fungal spray may help. To prevent the problem from recurring, be sure to collect fallen leaves and dispose of them immediately.

Sunburn

Description Black or black-edged patches on leaves can indicate sunburn. The leaves of some of the *Odontoglossum* purebred hybrids can become red during the summer.

Cause Black patches occur when the sun has shone directly on a portion of leaf for too long; it takes less than an hour for the sun to burn the leaves. A little redness in odontoglossums is acceptable, but if they receive too much sun, the leaves will suffer and be prematurely shed.

Cure Once burned, the mark will remain. Prevent sunburn by sheltering plants from the sun, particularly in spring, when the plants are still in their winter quarters and the sun is becoming increasingly bright.

Black rot

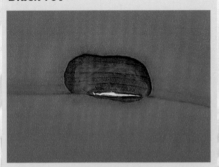

Description Rot that affects pseudobulbs can be dry or wet. When an older bulb at the back of a plant shrivels and turns brown, it is dying naturally. Where rot occurs in one or all of the newer pseudobulbs, affected pseudobulbs will turn brown and wet. This rot starts at the base of a pseudobulb and will run through the plant. Cattleyas and miltoniopsis are particularly susceptible.

Cause Rot in new pseudobulbs is caused by overwatering or by the plant remaining in a sodden state for a long time. Rot can also start in the new growth if water has lodged among the leaves and remained there for some time.

Cure Cut away the affected pseudobulbs to save the front part of the plant. Do this by cutting through the rhizome, discarding the diseased part of the plant, and dipping the remaining portion in a fungicide solution. Allow the plant to dry completely before potting it in a smaller pot. Treat wet rot in leaves by dusting the affected part with powdered sulfur.

Viruses

Description A virus infection often appears in young leaves as white streaking, either parallel to the vein or showing a defined diamond pattern along the length of the leaf. On broad-leaved orchids, such as phalaenopsis and cattleyas, a virus appears as black pitting on the leaf.

As the foliage ages, the damaged areas turn completely black, the result of a secondary infection coming into the leaf to survive in the dead leaf cells. The blackened areas are often the first noticeable sign of leaf-cell damage, and within a short time the virus will spread through the whole plant.

Cause Botanists believe that viruses are present in all plants, but only manifest themselves when a plant is weakened and not growing strongly. Orchids with a virus infection are usually unhealthy before the virus strikes, so they are under stress and less able to resist attack.

Cure The only remedy is to discard the plant before the virus spreads to other plants.

Yellow leaves

Description From time to time, the oldest leaves on a plant will turn yellow and drop off. This is a natural process. Where all the leaves take on a yellow shade of green, a nitrogen deficiency may be present.

Cause Nitrogen deficiency can be the result of insufficient nutrients in the compost. It may be old and used up or have decomposed. The problem can also be caused by not feeding the plant enough while it was growing.

Exposure to too much light also causes overall yellowing of the foliage. This seldom occurs indoors and is more likely to happen when orchids are grown in a greenhouse with inadequate shading. Cymbidiums placed outdoors for the summer can also turn yellow if they are left in too bright a position.

Cure Repot if new compost is necessary, and allow the plant to establish a new root system before applying a nitrogen-based feed at regular intervals of every second or third watering. While waiting for new roots to develop, give a regular foliar feed once every two weeks, misting the foliage so that minute water droplets cover the leaves like dew. This will return the foliage to a healthy green. Again, nitrogen feeding will help.

pest control

Most pests that attack orchids are sapsuckers, but some may chew leaves and roots. They are usually small and can often remain undetected until a large colony has developed.

Often the damage caused by insect pests is the first noticeable sign of an infestation. All the sap-sucking pests mentioned here can be eradicated by the use of rubbing alcohol, which kills on contact, but you have to be persistent to ensure that all generations present are wiped out. At any time, both adult and young, including eggs, will inhabit the colony, so you will need several sessions to get rid

Mealybugs

A mealybug is a soft-bodied insect about 1/10 inch (3 mm) long. The bug is oval, with two long filaments at the rear, and the whole body is covered in a soft, white mealy substance. It is wingless and moves by crawling. It feeds by sucking sap from all parts of the plant, causing stunted growth and yellow leaves. The bugs can be solitary or gather in clusters, and where you find one, you may discover that a colony is not far away. Check every part of the plant, including the flowers, particularly on phalaenopsis. Mealybugs lay their eggs underneath leaves and the grubs feed among the leaves.

Cure To remove the bugs on flowers, dab them with a cotton swab or a small paintbrush dipped in rubbing alcohol. If the plants are not in bloom, spray them with insecticidal soap, available in garden centers.

Scale

Scale insects differ in shape—they may be round or oblong—and coloring. Hard scale is brownish, while soft scale is white and cottony-looking. The insects are tiny, usually about 5/64 inch (2 mm) across.

Hard scale protects itself with a scaly membrane that covers the insect and under which the females lay their eggs. The young hatchlings are active and move away to colonize other plants. The adults remain stationary, usually underneath the leaves, and cause yellow patches on them. Soft scale excretes a sugary honeydew on which sooty mold can grow.

Look out for the insects particularly on cattleyas, where they hide behind the sheaths of the pseudobulbs, causing brown patches. Undetected scale will be densely packed in large colonies.

Cure To kill scale, the insect must be dislodged. Use a toothbrush dipped in rubbing alcohol to brush it off the plant. Scale can be hidden on cattleyas. To find it, routinely peel away all the dried bracts that cover the rhizome, as well as the pseudobulbs. Done carefully, this will not harm the plant.

Red Spider Mites

These orange-colored mites are extremely small—about half the size of a pinhead—and you will often need a magnifying glass to see them and the fine webs they create. Look on the undersides of the leaves, particularly of cymbidiums. Otherwise, take a white paper tissue and run it along the underside of the leaf; any mites that are rubbed off will show up more readily on the paper.

The pest causes large silvery white areas where it has sucked the leaf cells dry; this is often the first sign that red spider mites are present. In time, the silvery areas will turn black, and the damaged leaves will not become green again.

Cure Dispose of badly damaged leaves and clean off mites and webbing from those not too badly affected. Spider mites thrive in a hot, dry atmosphere, so improve the growing conditions for the orchid by increasing humidity and ventilation.

of them. Wearing disposable gloves, take a soft paper towel dipped in rubbing alcohol and wipe every part of the plant. These pests are also a major cause of the spread of viruses and other diseases in orchids. As they move about, they can carry diseases from plant to plant.

Many chemical pesticides are available to control the pests, including systemic insecticides, but when growing orchids in the home, don't resort to chemicals unless gentler methods have failed. These include washing and spraying with natural oils and insect traps. When using chemical pesticides, put the plants outdoors or in a garage or shed for the duration of treatment. Take care with all chemicals, some of which can do further harm to orchids— read the instructions and follow them carefully.

Aphids

Aphids, commonly known as greenfly, whitefly, and blackfly, are slow-moving insects that breed extremely rapidly to create large colonies. Aphids can do great harm to young growths and buds, causing distortion and yellowing of leaves. They are easily seen when in large numbers. Aphids excrete drops of honeydew, a sweet liquid that is attractive to ants, and the presence of ants will often alert you to the problem of aphids on a plant. If left, the honeydew will cause sooty mold to grow.

Cure Aphids can be easily destroyed by washing the plant in a bucket of water. Swill the plant, gently agitating the affected part, until all the insects are shaken free.

Excretions of honeydew also need to be cleaned off with a soft, wet cloth.

Ants, attracted by the aphids' honeydew, do little harm unless they decide to nest in the compost. If this happens, use ant traps or soak the plant to remove the ants.

Fungus gnats and springtails

These tiny insects can be harmful when they form large infestations. Fungus gnats lay their eggs in the compost, where the grubs live on decaying matter and accelerate the breakdown of the compost. Springtails are wingless insects that live around the surface of the compost and under pots and also cause the compost to deteriorate.

Cure Fungus gnats can be controlled by placing a few insect-trapping sticky strips close by, or by using sticky-leaved plants such as sundews (*Drosera* spp.) or butterworts (*Pinquicula* spp.) above, to trap them.

The best way to deal with springtails is to kill off the larvae, which live in the compost, by adding insecticide when watering.

Slugs and Snails

These common predators are easy to spot, but don't underestimate them, particularly when orchids are kept outdoors. Slugs and snails can do a lot of harm by eating through flower spikes and gnawing holes in pseudobulbs. There is no part of an orchid they will not attack. Since they are most active at night, the best time to look for them is after dark, using a flashlight to shine through sheaths and bracts where they often hide to feed unseen.

Cure If you do not want to resort to slug killer, lay pieces of potato or apple slices on the surface of the compost to trap slugs and snails. Small bush snails, in particular, are easily caught by this method. Remember to check the potato or apple slices each morning to gather up and dispose of the predators underneath.

the right water

When we water our plants, we assume that we are providing exactly what they require, but this is not always the case.

Most cultivated orchids derive from epiphytes. In the wild, they grow on trees and never come into contact with the ground, relying instead entirely on the rain for life-giving moisture.

In parts of the world where rainfall is scarce but orchids are common, such as cloud forests, the orchids are sustained by the high humidity and the moisture-laden clouds that leave the plants enshrouded every morning in a heavy dew.

Whether they live in rain forests or cloud forests, all the tree-growing orchids store water in their pseudobulbs, thick, succulent leaves, and roots to sustain them through periods of drought.

Orchid growers once grew their plants in *Sphagnum* moss, which thrives in extremely acid peat bogs. They used to say that if the moss was growing around the base of the orchid, then the orchid was happy. This practice has, however, long been discontinued by most modern growers, mainly on ecological grounds. Today growers use more scientific methods to be sure the orchids are getting the right water.

When growing orchids at home, don't assume that you can water them with whatever water is available. Rainwater that has been collected in a water barrel is the ideal. But in dry areas where it seldom rains, or for people living in apartments, rainwater will not be easy to get.

Straight from the faucet?

Tap water varies considerably. Local water authorities produce this commodity to a standard suitable for human consumption, but this does not necessarily mean that it is ideal for orchids!

The source of your tap water determines its suitability for orchids. When it has fallen as rain on mountains and been stored in reservoirs before being delivered directly to your house, it may be all right to use it. If, however, the water has come out of the ground, where it has been for hundreds or thousands of years, it will contain many salts and other minerals. This water may not be suitable for

MAKING SOFT WATER

If you do not have a ready source of soft water, you can make your own. Homemade water softeners are easily produced.

Fill a large bucket or tub with tap water and fill a nylon stocking or a plastic mesh bag with peat or horticultural charcoal. Suspend this bag in the bucket of water for a few days and the acidity of the water will greatly improve.

Nestled in a crevice beside a waterfall in a tropical garden, this *Dendrobium* hybrid is flourishing.

orchids. The same may be true of water that has been drawn from rivers or natural springs, especially where it has come from limestone deposits, when its alkalinity can be very high—well above 7pH, which is neutral. The ideal acidity for orchids is between 5.5 and 6.5pH, which is known as soft water. Your local water authority will be able to tell you if your water is soft or hard.

Finding soft water

So where are you going to find a regular source of soft water if you live in a place where either it doesn't rain or where you are unable to collect the rainwater? Bottled water from the supermarket may appear at first to be the ideal solution, but just as tap water varies, so does bottled water. Each manufacturer claims to have the best because it contains all sorts of healthful minerals, but these minerals may well be detrimental to your plants.

There are other ways to source soft water. Boiling tap water or bottled water will extract most of the impurities and leave better-quality water. Many kinds of water softeners are available. Some of them add salts to the water to improve its quality, but these salts can be harmful to your orchids. The best water softeners are those that use a process called reverse osmosis—these methods do not use any chemicals and produce unlimited supplies of fresh, clear water that are fine for orchids.

how to water orchids

Soft water for your orchids is critical, as is the water temperature, where you store the water, and the way you water your plants.

Water should be kept at the same temperature as the orchids. If it is stored outdoors or in a garage or shed, especially in winter, it is likely to give the orchids a chill and slow their growth. Let it rise to room temperature before using it.

In some places, soft water is not readily available, and the supply for watering your orchids needs to be stored and used carefully. Making the most of the little soft water you have may be achieved by dipping your plants rather than watering them directly at the rim of the pot. But keep in mind that

recycling water this way is not always a good idea. For instance, if you have a sick plant that has a virus infection in its roots, the infection will be spread from plant to plant if you reuse the water.

If you water your plants once or twice with hard tap water it will not instantly harm them, but if it is used constantly, the acidity of the compost will gradually change until it becomes unsuitable for the plants' roots. In such circumstances you may need to repot your plants annually.

Underwatering

When orchids are growing, they need to be kept evenly moist, avoiding the two extremes of total dryness and saturation. It is easy to go from one extreme to the other, and orchids usually suffer from underwatering when you are afraid of overwatering. While they are resting, orchids can go for several weeks in an almost completely dry state, but while they are growing, they need moisture at the roots.

An underwatered plant will feel light when you pick it up, and it will have shriveled pseudobulbs or, with a *Phalaenopsis* or *Vanda*, dehydrated and limp or creased foliage. Give the plant a good soaking for half an hour or so in a bucket of water, and then spray or mist the foliage and aerial roots several times daily until the plant has recovered. As soon as the plant feels light again, give it a normal watering. Continue with spraying and regular watering until the pseudobulbs or leaves plump up.

Underwatering is more likely to occur when a plant needs to be repotted and there is little space left in the pot for the water to penetrate. Although you may be watering regularly, most of the water will run off the surface, with little reaching the roots. In this situation, dip the plant until you can repot it into a larger pot. The growth of underwatered plants will be slowed, and not until a plant has recovered its moisture reserves will it start to grow normally.

Laden with dew, this *Brassia* dwelling high in the cloud forest takes in plenty of water.

Dip bark-mounted orchids every now and again so that they get a thorough soaking.

Spray bark-mounted orchids daily. This helps to keep the plant fresh and active and exposed aerial roots growing well.

ADDING FERTILIZER

Since orchid compost does not contain many nutrients—Rockwool, in fact, is sterile and contains none—you will need to add fertilizer from time to time when watering. See orchid entries for specific details.

Dip pot-bound orchids so that water can soak into the roots rather than run off.

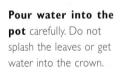

Pour water into the pot carefully. Do not splash the leaves or get water into the crown.

Overwatering

A plant has been overwatered when it has become saturated at the roots, with the result that the roots rot and die. Often the first sign of root loss is shriveling of the pseudobulbs; but unlike the underwatered plant, this one feels very heavy when it is picked up. In this instance, the pseudobulbs have shriveled because, without roots to sustain them, they have lost most of their moisture and cannot replace it.

If you suspect that the plant has been overwatered, take it out of its pot and look at the roots. You will find the roots blackened and dead, and probably very wet, in sodden compost. First, allow the plant to dry out, then reduce the number of pseudobulbs to those with some foliage, and cut away all dead roots. Repot the plant into as small a pot as possible, with fresh bark compost. Even if the plant does not die from shock, it can take several years for it to recover.

glossary

Aerial root
A root growing outside the pot that takes moisture from the air.

Adventitious growths
New growths that come from the stem or partway along a cane.

Alliance
A term used to describe closely related orchid genera.

Backbulb
The oldest, usually leafless pseudobulb.

Bark compost
Bark chips obtained from forestry trees after felling.

Bifoliate
A term used to describe an orchid within the *Cattleya* Alliance that produces two leaves on each pseudobulb.

Bigeneric hybrid
A man-made hybrid where two related genera are crossed.

Bulbil
A small adventitious growth that usually appears at the apex of a pseudobulb, most often on pleiones.

Cane
An elongated pseudobulb, as produced by dendrobiums.

Clone
A plant that is identical to others that have been mass-produced.

Column
A fingerlike structure at the center of an orchid flower that contains the plant's reproductive parts.

Cool temperature
A range of 50°F (10°C) to 75°F (24°C).

Crown
The center of a rosette of leaves of a monopodial orchid.

Dorsal sepal
The sepal that appears at the top of the flower.

Dropping on
A method of potting without disturbing the root ball. The plant is dropped into a larger pot.

Epiphyte
An orchid that grows naturally upon trees as an air plant but does not harm the tree by sapping nutrients from it.

Eye
Horticultural name for a dormant node on the flower spike of a phalaenopsis or a soft-caned dendrobium.

Foliar feed
Liquid fertilizer that is sprayed on the leaves, rather than applied when watering the plant.

Honey guide
The marks on the lip of an orchid that guide pollinating insects into the center of the flower.

Horticultural foam
Rubber-based spongy material used in orchid compost.

Horticultural soap
A soap used in controlling sap-sucking pests.

Humidity tray
A tray containing water that is placed beneath an orchid to create moisture in a dry atmosphere.

Hybrid grex
A term used to describe a group of plants, all of which have the same parents.

Intergeneric hybrid
A man-made hybrid containing three or more related genera.

Intermediate temperature
A range of 55°F (13°C) to 86°F (30°C).

Keiki
A small adventitious growth formed on the orchid stem or on the apex of a pseudobulb.

Labellum
Also known as the lip, the third, or central, petal of an orchid.

Lithophyte
A plant that grows on rock in the same way as an epiphyte grows on trees.

Mericloning
A method of mass-producing orchids using laboratory techniques.

Meristemmed plants
Orchids produced by artificial methods; all will be identical.

Monopodial
A term applied to an orchid with a single shoot that grows upward from a central stem or rhizome.

Multigeneric hybrid
The same as an intergeneric hybrid.

Multi-leaded
Term used to describe a plant that has produced two or more new growths at a time.

New growth
A newly maturing pseudobulb or growth in its early stages of development.

Node
A joint or notch on a stem from which buds or new leaves will grow.

Perlag
An ingredient used to open up orchid compost and and keep it aerated.

Perlite
A material with a similar purpose to Perlag. It is finer than Perlag.

Petal
All orchid flowers have three petals, the central one of which is modified into the labellum, or lip.

Pollinia
Waxy clumps of orchid pollen that are formed into two or more small masses.

Pseudobulb
A swollen stem that serves to retain water; it is not a true bulb.

Resting
A term applied to an orchid that is not actively growing and is in a dormant state.

Rhizome
A horizontal, ever-extending often underground stem from which new or vertical pseudobulbs grow.

Rockwool
An inorganic man-made material used in potting as an alternative type of compost.

Sepal
Behind the three petals on an orchid are three sepals that usually look similar to the petals.

Sequential flowering
A term used to describe orchids that have a succession of flowers rather than flowers that open all at once.

Stamen
The male part of the flower that carries the pollen.

Stigma
The female part of the flower. In orchids it is a small sticky depression under the column that receives the pollen.

Sympodial
A term applied to an orchid that grows from a pseudobulb or from the rhizome of a previous growth.

Terrestrial
An orchid that grows in the ground or in leaf litter (rotted fallen leaves) rather than on trees or rocks.

Unifoliate
A term used to describe an orchid within the *Cattleya* Alliance that bears a single leaf on each pseudobulb.

resources

Societies

The American Orchid Society
16700 A.O.S. Lane
Delray Beach, FL
33446
Tel: (561) 404-2000
www.orchidweb.org

The Canadian Orchid Congress
is the association of all Canadian
orchid societies.
www.canadianorchidcongress.ca

Orchid Society of Great Britain
www.orchid-society-gb.com

North of England Orchid Society
www.orchid.org.uk/neos

U. S. Suppliers:

Cal-Orchid, Inc.
1251 Orchid Drive
Santa Barbara, CA
93111
Tel: (805) 967-1312
www.calorchid.com

Carter and Holmes Orchids
629 Mendenhall Road
P.O. Box 668
Newberry, SC
29108
Tel: (803) 276-0579
www.carterandholmes.com

Orchidarium, Inc.
1229 South Sixth Street
Minneapolis, MN
55415
Tel: (612) 333-0155
www.orchidarium.com

Orchids by Hausermann, Inc.
2N134 Addison Road
Villa Park, IL
60181
Tel: (630) 543-6855
www.orchidsbyhausermann.com

Palmer Orchids
1308 Broadway Avenue
Pasadena, TX
77506
Tel: (713) 472-1364
www.flash.net/~palmerr/

Parkside Orchid Nursery
2503 Mountain View Drive
Ottsville, PA
18942
Tel: (610) 847-8039
www.parksideorchids.com

Canadian Suppliers:

Paramount Orchids
1060 - 101 Street SW
Calgary AB T3H 3Z5
Tel: (403) 686-7021
www.paramountorchids.com

Oriental Orchids
6039 12th Avenue
Burnaby BC V3N 2J2
Tel: (604) 515-7133
www.oriental-orchids.com

The Cypripedium Garden
17 Ready Way
Nepean ON K2J 2R7
Tel: (613) 825-1315
www.infonet.ca/cypr

Windsor Greenhouse
RR 2, 345 Gabriel Road
Falmouth NS B0P 1L0
Tel: (902) 798-0514
www.users.eastlink.ca/~greenhouses

index

picture credits and acknowledgments

PICTURE CREDITS

Abbreviations:
T=Top; M=Middle; B=Bottom;
R=Right; L=Left

All photographs are by Derek Cranch with the exception of the following:

p. 7 Red Cover/Linda Burgess, BL; pp. 8–9 The Garden Picture Library/Pernilla Bergdahl. p. 14 Robert Jacobs/Orchidarum Inc. p. 16 The Garden Picture Library/Pernilla Bergdahl. p. 20 The Garden Picture Library/Friedrich Strauss, TR; Gerald Cubitt, BR. p. 25 The Garden Picture Library/Friedrich Strauss, T. p. 40 Gerald Cubitt. p. 43 The Garden Picture Library/Lynne Brotchie, BL. p. 58 The Garden Picture Library/Pernilla Bergdahl. p. 74 The Garden Picture Library/Friedrich Strauss, TR; Nature Picture Library/Tim Shepherd, BR. p. 77 The Garden Picture Library/Friedrich Strauss. p. 79 The Garden Picture Library/Linda Burgess, R. p. 90 Ian Armitage. p. 100 OSF. p. 108 The Garden Picture Library/Pernilla Bergdahl, TR; OSF/Caroline Brett, BR. p. 124 The Garden Picture Library/Pernilla Bergdahl, TR; Gerald Cubitt, BR. p. 145 Gerald Cubitt. p. 148

The Garden Picture Library/Pernilla Bergdahl. pp. 164–65 Red Cover/Linda Burgess. p. 166 The Garden Picture Library/Pernilla Bergdahl, BR. p. 172 Red Cover/Graham Atkins-Hughes, TR; Red Cover/Andreas von Einsiedel, B. p. 173 The Garden Picture Library/Pernilla Bergdahl. pp. 178–79 Gerald Cubitt. p. 183 Nature Picture Library/Bengt Lundberg. p. 184 OSF/Michael Fogden.
Back Cover: Clockwise, The Garden Picture Library, Pernilla Bergdahl, 5.

ACKNOWLEDGMENTS

Toucan Books would also like to thank the following for their assistance in the preparation of this book: Nick Armitage, John Craven, and Sara Rittershausen and the staff of Burnham Nurseries.
  With special thanks to Lombok (www.lombok.co.uk) for the loan of the pots and containerss shown on pages 17, 41, 75, 101, 125, and 137, and to Birgit Blitz for the pots on pages 59 and 109.